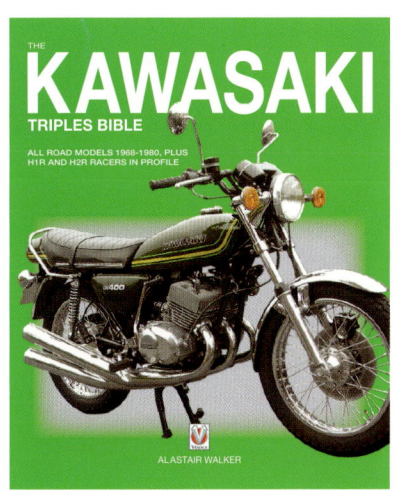

Other great books from Veloce –

Speedpro Series
Harley-Davidson Evolution Engines – How to Build & Power Tune (Hammill)
Motorcycle-engined Racing Car – How to Build (Pashley)

Those Were The Days ... Series
Café Racer Phenomenon, The (Walker)
Drag Bike Racing in Britain – From the mid '60s to the mid '80s (Lee)
Three Wheelers (Bobbitt)

Essential Buyer's Guide Series
BMW GS (Henshaw)
BSA Bantam (Henshaw)
BSA 500 & 650 Twins (Henshaw)
Harley-Davidson Big Twins (Henshaw)
Hinckley Triumph triples & fours 750, 900, 955, 1000, 1050, 1200 – 1991-2009 (Henshaw)
Honda CBR600 (Henshaw)
Honda FireBlade (Henshaw)
Honda SOHC fours 1969-1984 (Henshaw)
Norton Commando (Henshaw)
Triumph Bonneville (Henshaw)
Vespa Scooters – Classic 2-stroke models 1960-2008 (Paxton)

Auto-Graphics Series
Lambretta Li Series Scooters (Sparrow)

General
Bluebird CN7 (Stevens)
BMW Boxer Twins 1970-1995 Bible, The (Falloon)
British 250cc Racing Motorcycles (Pereira)
BSA Bantam Bible, The (Henshaw)
Ducati 750 Bible, The (Falloon)
Ducati 750 SS 'round-case' 1974, The Book of the (Falloon)
Ducati 860, 900 and Mille Bible, The (Falloon)
Edward Turner: The Man Behind the Motorcycles (Clew)
Fine Art of the Motorcycle Engine, The (Peirce)
Funky Mopeds (Skelton)
Lambretta Bible, The (Davies)
Laverda Twins & Triples Bible 1968-1986 (Falloon)
Moto Guzzi Sport & Le Mans Bible, The (Falloon)
Motorcycle Apprentice (Cakebread)
Motorcycle Road & Racing Chassis Designs (Noakes)
Off-Road Giants! – Heroes of 1960s Motorcycle Sport (Westlake)
Redman, Jim – 6 Times World Motorcycle Champion: The Autobiography (Redman)
Scooters & Microcars, The A-Z of Popular (Dan)
Scooter Lifestyle (Grainger)
Singer Story: Cars, Commercial Vehicles, Bicycles & Motorcycle (Atkinson)

Triumph Bonneville!, Save the – The inside story of the Meriden Workers' Co-op (Rosamond)
Triumph Motorcycles & the Meriden Factory (Hancox)
Triumph Speed Twin & Thunderbird Bible (Woolridge)
Triumph Tiger Cub Bible (Estall)
Triumph Trophy Bible (Woolridge)
Velocette Motorcycles – MSS to Thruxton New Third Edition (Burris)

From Veloce Publishing's new imprints:

Soviet General & field rank officer uniforms: 1955 to 1991 (Streather)
Red & Soviet military & paramilitary services: female uniforms 1941-1991 (Streather)

Clever Dog! (O'Meara)
Complete Dog Massage Manual, The – Gentle Dog Care (Robertson)
Dinner with Rover (Paton-Ayre)
Dog Cookies (Schops)
Dog Games – Stimulating play to entertain your dog and you (Blenski)
Dogs on wheels (Mort)
Dog Relax – Relaxed dogs, relaxed owners (Pilguj)
Exercising your puppy: a gentle & natural approach (Robertson)
Know Your Dog – The guide to a beautiful relationship (Birmelin)
Living with an Older Dog (Alderton & Hall)
My dog has cruciate ligament injury – but lives life to the full! (Häusler)
My dog has hip dysplasia – but lives life to the full! (Häusler)
My dog is blind – but lives life to the full! (Horsky)
My dog is deaf – but lives life to the full! (Willms)
Smellorama – nose games for dogs (Theby)
Swim to Recovery: Canine hydrotherapy healing (Wong)
Waggy Tails & Wheelchairs (Epp)
Walkin' the dog – Motorway walks for dogs and drivers (Rees)
Winston ... the dog who changed my life (Klute)
You and Your Border Terrier – The Essential Guide (Alderton)
You and Your Cockapoo – The Essential Guide (Alderton)
You and Your Cockapoo – The Essential Guide (Alderton)

www.veloce.co.uk

First published in November 2010 by Veloce Publishing Limited, Veloce House, Parkway Farm Business Park, Middle Farm Way, Poundbury, Dorchester, Dorset, DT1 3AR, England.
Fax 01305 250479/e-mail info@veloce.co.uk/web www.veloce.co.uk or www.velocebooks.com.

ISBN: 978-1-845840-75-4 UPC: 6-36847-04075-8

© Alastair Walker and Veloce Publishing 2010. All rights reserved. With the exception of quoting brief passages for the purpose of review, no part of this publication may be recorded, reproduced or transmitted by any means, including photocopying, without the written permission of Veloce Publishing Ltd. Throughout this book logos, model names and designations, etc, have been used for the purposes of identification, illustration and decoration. Such names are the property of the trademark holder as this is not an official publication.
Readers with ideas for automotive books, or books on other transport or related hobby subjects, are invited to write to the editorial director of Veloce Publishing at the above address.
British Library Cataloguing in Publication Data – A catalogue record for this book is available from the British Library. Typesetting, design and page make-up all by Veloce Publishing Ltd on Apple Mac.
Printed in India by Replika Press. Front cover picture courtesy of Lee Doxey.

THE KAWASAKI TRIPLES BIBLE

ALL ROAD MODELS 1968-1980, PLUS H1R AND H2R RACERS IN PROFILE

Veloce Publishing
THE PUBLISHER OF FINE AUTOMOTIVE BOOKS

Contents

Introduction and acknowledgements 5
Chapter one – Before the triples 8
Chapter two – The H1 500 series 20
Chapter three – KH500 42
Chapter four – The H2 series 48
Chapter five – The 350 S2 series 65
Chapter six – The 400 S series 76
Chapter seven – KH400 series 81
Chapter eight – The 250 S series 89
Chapter nine – KH250 series 1976-81 99
Chapter ten – The racers 111
Chapter eleven – The H2R racers 126
Chapter twelve – Le Coupe Sportif 139
Chapter thirteen – The UK KH400 race series 144
Index 159

Introduction and acknowledgements

The Kawasaki triples remain some of the most collectable examples of Japanese motorcycles from the late '60s/early '70s boom years; an era when Japan turned motorcycling from a low budget method of transportation into a sexy, high speed leisure pursuit. Kawasaki's ad agency in the USA hit the nail on the head with its 'Let the good times roll' slogan.

Starting with the H1 of 1968, Kawasaki produced a range of beautifully-styled, unique-sounding, high-performance, three cylinder motorbikes, aimed squarely at younger consumers with a passion for speed and acceleration. These were machines that 'kicked ass on the quarter mile,' as the Americans say. These violent, noisy, smoking two-strokes were intended as the two-wheeled equivalents to the Ford Mustangs, AC Cobras, and Ferrari Daytonas of their time. The fact that the triples didn't handle corners too well, and drank fuel like there was no tomorrow, made little difference to H1 and H2 fans.

From late '71, Kawasaki launched a succession of triples to join its original fire-breathing 500; the 750 H2, 350 S2, 250 S1, and later on the 400 S3 and KH series models. Success in the 500cc Grand Prix circus, AMA Championships, European and Australian endurance, plus various production road race series also proved the potential of the H1R and H2R competition models. But their reign was brief and they were soon overtaken by water-cooled two-strokes made first by Suzuki and then Yamaha.

Just as the 1980s began, the last of the road-based triples family, the novice level KH250, ceased production (the 750, 500 and 400 had already been deleted from the Kawasaki range). An incredible chapter in biking history had ended. The '70s really were the decade of the screaming two-stroke for many young riders, but emissions and noise legislation in Europe and the USA effectively finished off the air-cooled strokers.

Today, the Kawasaki triples have a dedicated fan base around the world, with the older 500- and 750-sized bikes the most prized by collectors and restorers. This book, however, is aimed at all triples enthusiasts, both classic bike collectors and those who simply have a passing interest in the Kawasaki three cylinder machines.

These motorcycles were crazy, irrational objects. Their impact was lasting. An Italian triples fan summed it up for me very well: "A CB750 was like your wife, but a H1 500 was your mistress."

Not politically correct, I know, but then

THE KAWASAKI TRIPLES BIBLE

Mimmi Cazzanigi, riding for Kawasaki Motor Italia at Imola in 1974. The machine is now owned by the Wafna race team. (Courtesy Lucio Cocchi)

neither were the triples. Long may they remain an echo of the raw, gutsy engineering that made Kawasaki one of the 'big four' manufacturers.

The elusive truth

This book was written for love, not money. After owning two triples and growing up with the bikes in the '70s, I have no illusions about them. The triples were fantastic looking, temperamental, noisy, thirsty, addictive machines that handled dubiously when pushed hard. If you can't handle basic truths like that, then this book may upset you.

Because of space limitations and the time I had available, I have concentrated on tracing the history of the triples in Europe and North America, with the UK obviously of major interest. There are two chapters on grass roots level Kawasaki racing, the French Coupe Kawasaki and UK KH400 Cup road race series. My thanks to Yves Evrard of Les Amis de la Coupe Kawasaki and Tony Jakeman in that respect.

I have tried to skim through the highlights of the H1R and H2R road racing history as well, but apologise in advance to the many retired road racers, mechanics and team managers who haven't had a chance to add their memories. Books have been written purely about the racing triples, and rightly so.

One immutable truth has emerged from my partial road racing research; nobody can buy an 'original' H1R or H2R with any degree of certainty. Almost every team or rider back then modified their machines, from the word go, in a desperate war of two-stroke attrition. That truth may not sit well in a glossy auction catalogue, but road racing during the late '60s/early '70s can be summed up in one pithy quote from an anonymous team member; "It was only cheating if you got caught."

As regards the road models, this book offers an incomplete but hopefully fair-minded history. It has been put together using the testimony of dealers, enthusiasts and racers who were there, or those who have a lifelong passion for the bikes today. There was also a vast archive of published material to sift through, some true, some myth.

Machine production numbers, colours offered in particular markets, or the exact dates when disc brakes superseded drums, are all educated guesses based on available evidence. The early expansion of Japanese motorcycle manufacturers was rapid; some might say buccaneering. Entrepreneurs went to Japan and bought Kawasaki triples for cash, sometimes official importers were bypassed. I do not believe that anyone can offer 100 per cent accurate figures on a market-by-market basis, since official records have either been shredded, or the information offered lacks credibility. This lack of accurate information about model distribution is frustrating for collectors and restorers alike, but realistically nobody at Kawasaki is going to offer a detailed breakdown of exactly what happened 30-40 years ago.

This is also a book about the full throttle world of motorcycling in the '70s. I have tried

KAWASAKI HISTORY

Adolfo Drago (yellow T-shirt) and members of the Italian rock band, Mach III, pictured in 1977. (Courtesy Adolfo Drago)

to capture the essence of a truly special time, when a generation of riders discovered the freedom of the roads, and some of the most fiery, sweet-sounding and bad-ass motorbikes ever made.

We will never see those days again; as a result the world is a safer, duller place.

Thanks department

Six months' solid work would have meant little without the assistance freely given by Kawasaki triple owners, forum members, ex-racers, technicians, Kawasaki employees past and present, and Kawasaki dealers. The enthusiasm for triples is ingrained within many people, like a tattoo indelibly etched in two-stroke oil.

First, let me mention those who helped make the book truly come alive as a project, without whose in-depth assistance and advice, it would not have been possible. Tony Jakeman at BMW GB, former organiser of the KH400 Cup; Rick Brett, the guru in the wooly hat; Yves Evrard and Les Amis de la Coupe Kawasaki; Bill Smith, from Bill Smith Motors, Chester; Kevin Cameron, former technician for various Kawasaki race teams; Chip Furlong, H1R racer back in the day; Ed Moran, Service Manager, Kawasaki East Coast; Dave Crussell, Kawasaki triples racer and collector; Malc Anderson, Kawa triples club UK.

I also appreciate the time and effort given by: Dave Matthews, former KH400 racer; Gary Nixon, legend; Heinz Ehmer, Kawasaki triples club Germany; Ton Pels, Zodiac International Netherlands; Dave Koup, Koups Motorcycles PA; Dave Chisma, former H2 proddie racer in Canada; Grant Hacking, Doug Hacking Motorcycles; Charlie Williams, former road racer; Johnny Doome, KH250 aficionado; Simon Lister, UK 250/350/400 triples specialist; Gary Bonella, KH250 owner; Mick Boddice, UK sidecar racer and race school owner; Simon Whitelock, the professor of Kawasaki specials; Jim Breslin, former Kawasaki Canada employee; Adolfo Drago, triple enthusiast in Italy; Allessandro Generotti, Italy; Kawasaki Tre Italy; Jan Olav Garvik, Kawa triples enthusiast in Norway; Mike Gardner Snr, USA; Terje Aspmo; Eric Offenstadt, H1R, H2, SMAC racer and engineer; Steve Brown UK; Willems Knol, Holland; Nigel Wynne, Vintage Bike UK; Abergavenny Motorcycles, Wales; Jeff Henise, USA; Dave and Gail, Melbourne; Chris Speight, KMSA; Bob Goddard, former MCM journalist; Paul Bell, UK; Atze, German triples fan; Yogi, triples fan UK.

Visit Veloce on the web – www.veloce.co.uk / www.velocebooks.com
Details of all books in print • Special offers • New book news • Gift vouchers • Forum

CHAPTER ONE

BEFORE THE TRIPLES

To understand how Kawasaki established itself as a manufacturer of high performance motorcycles, it is worth looking back at the dramatic rise of the company, and the Japanese motorcycle industry in general.

In 1945, Kawasaki Aircraft Company, like all former military suppliers in Japan, was forced by law to curtail aircraft production. During WWII, Kawasaki had made fighter aircraft and modified Daimler-Benz/Messerschmitt engines to improve performance. Although most people know of the Mitsubishi Zero, few know that Kawasaki made the only WWII fighter plane in Japan featuring a water-cooled engine, and generally rated as one of the best aircraft Japan made at the time.

After its defeat in WWII, Japan was not permitted to build warplanes: Kawasaki could make aircraft spares, or component parts only, once plans were approved by the occupying American administration. So Kawasaki diversified, and became involved in the general economic reconstruction of Japan, manufacturing anything from pots and pans to ocean-going ships. Many war economy goods were recycled; for example, airplane fuselage tail wheels were used on the first Silver Pigeon scooters produced by Mitsubishi, and magnets from the radio packs of Japanese soldiers found their way into motorcycle electrical systems.

Many pioneers, such as Soichiro Honda, began assembling basic mopeds and scooters in the late 1940s, as fuel was strictly rationed and people needed simple, 'fixable' transport. Soichiro Honda wasn't the only entrepreneur who spotted an opportunity, however, and Kawasaki began design work on its first motorcycle engine as far back as 1948, as well as supplying component parts to fledgling motorcycle companies in the late '40s and early '50s.

The Meihatsu toe in the water

Kawasaki, busy with a range of industrial projects in the early 1950s, could see an explosion in demand for transport as the economy boomed. It was time to test the market, which it did with the Meihatsu brand.

The KE-1 four-stroke, 148cc single and KH 250 four-stroke engines were launched in 1953, just as scooter and motorcycle production was skyrocketing. Japanese two-wheeler production jumped from just 470 units in 1946, to 24,000 by 1950, and 166,000 in 1953.

The next project for Meihatsu was a DKW/BSA Bantam type two-stroke motor,

Before the Triples

The Meihatsu 125 from the mid '50s was Kawasaki's first serious attempt at motorcycle production.

As work began at Kawasaki's new motorcycle production plant, Meguro – one of the oldest names in Japanese motorcycling, and a business partner of Kawasaki's since the 1930s – ran into trouble. Meguro had suffered a which was available in 60cc/90cc/125cc formats. The reason that Kawasaki, BSA, Yamaha and others all used the DKW two-stroke design in the '50s is that essentially it was 'copyright free,' being part of the compensation that Germany had to pay the Allies following the end of WWII. Meihatsu then launched its own complete machine in the mid 1950s, having failed to achieve success with an expensive scooter a few years earlier.

The Japanese motorcycle industry then was a feverish, ever-changing jigsaw of motorcycle assembly companies, plus engine, frame or other component manufacturers. Copying was rife, ruthless double-crossing the norm. Undercutting rivals to gain market share became common after the Korean War ended in 1953, and a brief recession caused the Japanese economy to slow. It was the kind of market where Soichiro Honda gambled his entire company on buying expensive machine tools and making his own bikes, rather than trusting local parts suppliers. The gamble paid off, although Honda only narrowly avoided bankruptcy in the mid '50s as hundreds of small, Japanese bike makers went bust ...

Kawasaki was big enough financially, and well diversified in its product base, to stay aloof from much of this blood-filled shark pool. But it had ambition beyond being a mere supplier of engines and the small capacity Meihatsu machines, and so set up a motorcycle R&D facility in 1959, just as the market was changing and the opportunity to export loomed on the horizon.

year-long labour strike, just after launching a new range of lightweight bikes which sold poorly. Taken together, these two blows effectively bankrupted the company. Meguro was a prestige brand, supplying the Japanese government with police bikes, and had raced at Sao Paulo in Brazil in 1954, alongside Honda. The Meguro name had a distinctive value in Japan, and commanded a high level of respect.

So Kawasaki bought stock in Meguro, eventually taking full control in 1964. The timing was perfect. In the late 1950s, the Japanese government encouraged companies to expand overseas, as it was plain to see that the 1960s would be a decade of personal transport – and not just in Japan. This was a window of opportunity for Kawasaki, which already had a range of heavy industrial products and services,

By the '60s Meihatsu bikes were being slowly transformed into something a little more modern.

THE KAWASAKI TRIPLES BIBLE

Top: The Kawasaki factory at Akashi in 1959.

Above: The motorcycle assembly line in 1961.

but owning a motorcycle brand would bring the same kind of publicity that Honda and Yamaha gained by making a product aimed at the younger consumer.

It took time to learn from the new Meguro motorcycle division, and Kawasaki had to work with what it had, so re-badged existing machines as Kawasaki-Meguro Works 175 and 250 singles, plus Meguro had a staid-looking, albeit well made, 500 T1 twin, which had long-term potential. Kawasaki could see some kudos in producing a large capacity model, essentially a Japanese 'government' motorcycle, designed to fill the gap left by Rikuo, which made Harley-esque 750cc twins for police or government departmental use, but went bankrupt in 1960. (By the way, Rikuo literally means 'Road King' in Japanese.)

It was very important for Kawasaki, which had lucrative government contracts, to keep the T-series 500 Meguro in production, then revamp it as the W1/W2 650cc twin for the 1960s and into the mid '70s. Someone had to supply government agencies with a genuinely Japanese-made, large capacity motorbike suitable for state occasions, like the 1964 Olympics, for example. It was a

BEFORE THE TRIPLES

From Red Tank to Blue Streak

Kawasaki's first successful attempt at making a name for itself was in the domestic off-road racing scene, big news across Japan in the early 60s, with companies such as Yamaha, Honda and Suzuki entering well publicised motocross events, speedway races, or one-off hill climbs.

The Ranger 170 was part of the four-stroke line-up that Kawasaki produced using the Meguro name.

The Red Tank 125 was a successful off-road competition machine; Kawasaki's first winner.

question of 'face,' or honour, as much as commercial sense, which meant a great deal in Japan at that time.

But as the 1960s dawned, Kawasaki needed to make a name for itself worldwide as a dynamic motorcycle brand, which was a problem as Honda, Tohatsu and Yamaha already had established international road racing teams. The answer lay in competition – but off-road. Luckily for Kawasaki, it had a superb 125cc two-stroke, designed in-house and launched in 1960 as the 125 B7, to act as the foundation stone of its motorcycle division.

In 1962, Kawasaki launched the B8 125, and in 63 the B8 M competition motocrosser, later known as the 'Red Tank' Kawasaki 125, appeared on dirt tracks. This won the 125cc Japanese MX Championship in its debut year, the publicity from which helped put Kawasaki on the map in Japan. The little 125 MX machine featured a 12bhp, piston ported two-stroke, single cylinder engine, and, whilst it had its roots in the old Meihatsu 125 of the mid 50s, it was a punchier, revvier machine, demonstrating that the input from Kawasaki's dedicated R&D facility had paid off.

Kawasaki set records at the Bonneville Salt Flats to underline the performance credentials of its new machines.

This small B8 125 was also exported to the USA, as Kawasaki had already opened a sales office in America in 1960, as soon as it took a share in Meguro. The off-road Kawasaki bikes were soon available in sizes ranging from 60cc to 125cc, and helped form the main marketing plank in the brand's expansion into the USA. The big Meguro twins went over as well, setting up Kawasaki's first overseas office in Los Angeles in 1964, because America was the number one overseas market for Kawasaki.

However, it rapidly became apparent that the homely Meguros weren't finding many USA buyers, especially the smaller 175 and 250cc four-stroke singles. So Kawasaki expanded its range of two-stroke motocrossers, planned to turn the Meguro T1 500 into the more powerful Kawasaki W1 650, and began development on feisty, all-new, 250/350 two-stroke twins to power the A1 Samurai and A7 Avenger: bold names for machines that were to be sold in nations that had fought Japan just 20 years before.

By 1966, Kawasaki was ready. It opened an East Coast sales/parts office in Chicago just as the W1 650 – the first large capacity Japanese bike to arrive in the USA – went on sale.

The 250cc Samurai was launched early in May '66 and built on the experience that Kawasaki had acquired in developing the small-sized motocross bikes. The Kawasaki 90cc junior class off-road racers of the early '60s – such as the J1 model – featured rotary disc valve induction, which was more fuel efficient than simple piston port induction. The disc valve technology had come to Japan from East Germany, when Ernst Degner defected from MZ's race team to join Suzuki. Whatever the legalities of using disc valves, Suzuki, Bridgestone, and Kawasaki all made the most of this more advanced system of managing a charge of gas and air inside a two-stroke engine.

The Samurai 250 A1 was an immediate sensation. Claimed peak power output was 31bhp@8000rpm, with a five speed gearbox and a fairly low, 7:1 compression ratio. It was conservatively styled, with kneepads on the gas tank, a two-tone saddle which bolted, rather than hinged, onto the sub-frame, plus enclosed forks and shock absorbers. It also had an oval-shaped instrument cluster, pretty similar to that of the Suzuki Super Six of the time. To prevent the Samurai's engine being unfeasibly wide, the alternator and ignition were housed directly behind the engine, with the two carbs and disc valve assemblies mounted at each end of the crankshaft.

The Samurai A1 made it to Europe in late '66, but very few were sold, mainly due to the haphazard importer and dealer appointment system that Kawasaki employed. This was in sharp contrast to

650 W2SS COMMANDER

350 A7 AVENGER

250 A1SS SAMURAI

BEFORE THE TRIPLES

KAWASAKI 350cc Avenger A-7
Suggested Price* $785.00

ENGINE
Type ..... 2 two-cycle twin, rotary valve
Displacement .... 338 cc
Compression ratio 7.0:1
Horsepower .... 40.5 at 7500 rpm
Torque .... 28.86 ft/lbs at 7000 rpm
Ignition .... coil and battery
Bore and stroke .... 62 by 56 mm

TRANSMISSION
Primary drive .... gear
Type .... five speed foot operated
Clutch .... wet, multi plate

BRAKING DISTANCE
30MPH
60MPH

FRAME
Type .... double down tube
Front suspension ..... telehydraulic fork
Rear suspension .... telehydraulic shock
Brakes .... internal expanding

DIMENSIONS
Overall length .... 78.9 inches
Overall height .... 42.7 inches
Wheelbase .... 51.0 inches
Weight .... 329 pounds
Ground clearance .... 6.5 inches

PERFORMANCE
Quarter mile time ...... 15.7 seconds
Quarter mile speed .... 81.44 mph

5th .. 0.78:1
4th .. 0.92:1
3rd .. 1.13:1
2nd .. 1.53:1
1st .. 2.50:1
Neutral

*Retail (POE West Coast)

---

a cheaper option than a full factory works effort, which was horrendously expensive, as Honda was discovering by the mid '60s. Essentially a mildly tuned Samurai, the A1R had a claimed 40bhp from the higher compression motor; bigger, 26mm Mikuni carbs; magneto ignition; close ratio gearbox; new primary drive gears; expansion chamber exhausts, and a full fairing. The R version also featured two steering dampers, rather than the road-going Samurai A1's single headstock damper.

The A1-R 250 wasn't quite as successful as a production racer as was expected, with British riders like the late Dave Simmonds telling the motorcycle press that "... the gear ratios are too widely spaced."

This 1967 ad lists the 350 Avenger's quarter mile time as a sluggish 15.7 seconds. It may have used the 250's time in error.

In this ad the quarter mile has dropped to 13.8 seconds, and Kawasaki stresses the aircraft quality manufacture and 12 month warranty – a novelty back in the '60s.

the US market, but European racers were quick to warm to the potential of the Samurai's A1R clubman racer model, launched in December 1966 for the '67 road race season.

Road racing was much more important in Europe than the USA, and the 250 class was fiercely competitive, even at club level. Launching a 'kitted' race bike was also

THE KAWASAKI TRIPLES BIBLE

Below, left: "For people who know what it's all about!" wasn't the most memorable catchphrase in '60s copywriting.

Below, right: Using road racers to promote sporty motorcycles was an integral part of selling bikes back in the '60s. Kawasaki pioneered the contingency prize money idea, rather than fund a specific factory race team for the 250/350 twins.

Simmonds wasn't happy with the handling, either, and commissioned a new frame for his A1-R in order to claim 2nd place at Brands Hatch in '67. The A1-Rs reportedly suffered a succession of piston-holing problems, too.

Later in '67, the Avenger A7 twin cylinder road bike was launched, with a 338cc engine closely based on the original Samurai 250. Essentially, it was bored out to 62mm, from the 250's 53mm cylinder width. Bigger, 28mm Mikuni carbs helped the 350 Avenger breathe better and probably achieve the genuine 'ton' that the 250 Samurai was said to do. Claimed peak power was 40bhp and dry weight was 329lb, up just 10lb on the 250 Samurai.

Both the Samurai and Avenger twins helped establish Kawasaki as a performance brand in the USA, a manufacturer that was going places. The US marketing operation was much bigger than anything in Europe, and 'Street Scrambler' variants of the Samurai 250 and Avenger 350 (dubbed A1SS/A7SS) were released in 1967 purely for the US market. They were very successful in the US and Canada, but the A1/A7 SS twins were never officially imported to Europe in the late '60s. Kawasaki also signed a deal with McCormack/American Eagle to have the Big Horn, 350 Avenger, and other Kawasaki models restyled and sold as American Eagle machines in the USA. The venture wasn't a success and just eight 350 Avengers were sold as Eagles.

As 1968 progressed Kawasaki had two working prototypes of the motorcycles that would put the company well and truly on the map, one of which was the Mach III 500cc triple, codenamed Blue Streak. Close to completion was the four cylinder, 750cc, four-stroke flagship model, codenamed New York Steak. But word of Honda's imminent CB750 launch at the Tokyo show in autumn '68 reached Kawasaki, and the 750 four-stroke project was put on hold. For now, all of Kawasaki's energies would go into making the new 500cc H1 two-stroke

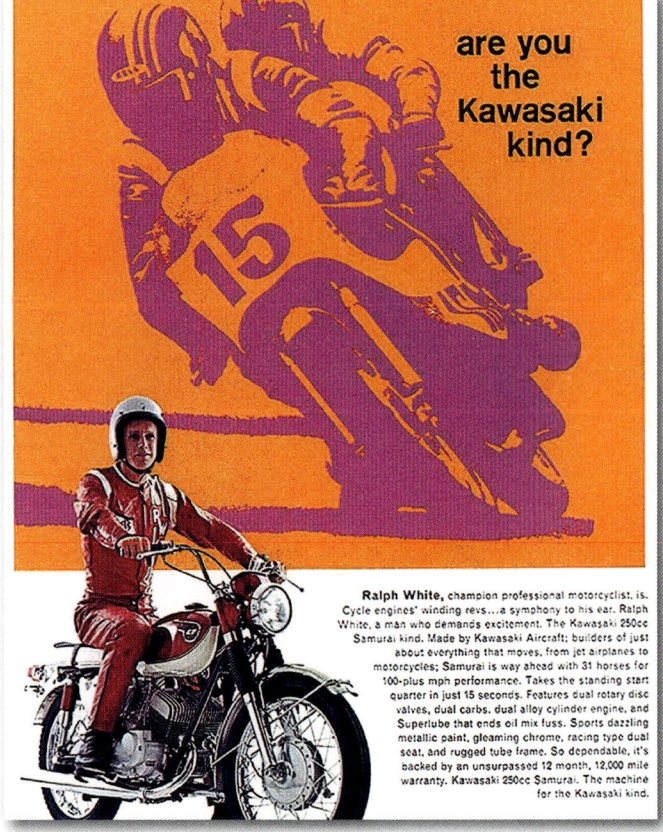

BEFORE THE TRIPLES

This restored Samurai 250 was admired at the Stafford Classic Motorcycle Show in 2009.

Kawasaki quickly learned to make its American market machines shiny, chrome-laden and featuring two-tone paintwork.

triple the basis of a complete new range of rapidly accelerating – and very eye-catching – road bikes.

The making of the Mach III

When Kawasaki's engineers sat down in 1964 to plan their 500cc masterpiece, the rationale behind project Blue Streak was simple; this would be a two-stroke road machine that was king of the quarter mile. A kick-ass hot-rod aimed at American riders who placed straight line acceleration above every other attribute. It might be nice if it was also the fastest production motorcycle in the world ...

A two-stroke triple cylinder engine wasn't unique, of course; DKW had started using a two-stroke in its cars back in 1928, and later, Saab modified the design and built an experimental V6 1500cc two-stroke in 1960. The DKW 750cc triple, which featured one ignition coil and a set of points per cylinder, was adapted for use in the Trabant and Wartburg cars produced under communist rule in East Germany.

Perhaps more interesting to Kawasaki was the use of the loop scavenging system on DKW engines as far back as the 1920s, plus the use of tuned DKW triples by Elva Junior racing cars in the '50s. A one-litre, ported DKW motor, with Dellorto or Amal carbs, was reputedly producing some 82bhp at 5500rpm. Also during the '50s, DKW pioneered the use of Telves fins on two-stroke engines, with the spacing and materials used offering better heat dissipation and noise reduction.

The German DKW company was a two-stroke evangelist, that single-handedly made the ring-ding engine a viable motorised power unit for motorcycles, no matter what Scott owners might think. Every decent Japanese two-stroke engine produced in the '50s and '60s is pretty much based on the DKW strokers, and refined using the knowledge accrued by those who raced them, which includes Kaaden and Degner, whose MZ racers of the '50s were essentially DKW engines breathing via disc valve induction.

So Kawasaki, like Yamaha, Tohatsu, Bridgestone, and Suzuki, started with DKW designs, and why not? The Germans were the best in the business. The 500 triple project got under way in earnest in 1966, once Kawasaki had put the finishing touches to its Samurai and Avenger twins.

Project Blue Streak was so vital to Kawasaki that it went headhunting, visiting Japanese universities to find the best engineers studying there. Soichiro Honda had done much the same in the '50s when recruiting talent, and Honda was a company in which two or three rival design teams, staffed mainly by graduates in their twenties, would compete to create a prototype ahead of their in-house rivals. Kawasaki took a similar approach with the Blue Streak project, giving two teams a blank sheet of paper. What capacity two-stroke would best produce 60bhp, with acceptable reliability? A 500, 650, maybe even a 750?

The thinking then was that any air-cooled, two-stroke twin much bigger than 500cc wouldn't survive being ridden hard over long distances without seizing up. DKW and Saab used large cooling fans on their car engines, but you couldn't do that on a motorcycle. So that set a theoretical capacity limit on any two cylinder motorcycle power unit, since bigger pistons meant more mass, friction – and therefore heat: how could iron cylinders dissipate that heat? Team one pursued the disc-valve, 500cc twin concept, a bigger version of the Avenger 350, essentially, and arguably the most cost-effective way forward in terms of manufacturing lines, tooling up, parts supply, etc.

Meanwhile, team two took the 500cc, air-cooled triple route, hoping that this might be the optimum power unit. A triple cylinder motor would also set the Kawasaki brand apart from Suzuki and Yamaha; both renowned for their stroker twins and well ahead of Kawasaki in terms of racing and international marketing by 1966.

But there was a twist to the three cylinder option. Kawasaki wondered if an L-shaped triple, with the centre cylinder pointing up, might provide better cooling than an in-line triple; plus, an L-shaped triple offered the option of using disc valve induction, rather than conventionally set carbs and piston port technology.

It was difficult for Kawasaki to decide, because, apart from its rivals' disc-valve, two-stroke racers winning at GP level, Kawasaki had fitted disc valves to the Samurai and Avenger, so wouldn't customers expect this technology on Blue Streak, too? The whole point of building a 500cc road bike was to sell Kawasaki as a performance brand, so even if an L-shaped triple looked odd, that wouldn't matter as long as it blasted past everything else on the dragstrip – and on the road.

Having shelved the 500cc twin idea, Kawasaki built two working prototypes of

BEFORE THE TRIPLES

The Avenger and Samurai were amongst the first Kawasaki machines imported to the UK during the mid '60s.

Below, left: The SS stood for 'Street Scrambler,' and these versions of the Samurai and Avenger were produced for the North American market only.

Below: Fiorino Cimatti on an A7R 350 race machine at the Bikers' Classics event, Spa Francorchamps circuit, 2009.

17

THE KAWASAKI TRIPLES BIBLE

the triple cylinder 500 motor, and headed off to Osaka university, where it carefully measured the cooling efficiency of the in-line and L-shaped variants whilst bench-testing the motors. A two-stroke engine needs a precise arrangement of cooling fins if it is to survive repeated high rpms, and the university's Faculty of Engineering looked at cylinder pitch, fin shape and spacing, and also monitored the various heat spots on both three cylinder prototypes. Although the L-shape ran a slightly cooler middle cylinder, the in-line triple was within acceptable limits, so Kawasaki went for that one. It's debatable whether an L-shaped triple – even a genuine 65bhp, 120mph one – would have held much aesthetic appeal to riders in the late '60s, but we will never know ...

Another feature of Blue Streak was the car-style CDI ignition, first seen on the A1 and A7 models, which fed more voltage to the sparkplugs. This helped create a 'fatter' spark, which in turn minimised unburnt gas in the combustion chamber. New sparkplugs, developed for use in the V-4, water-cooled, 125cc KR3 racer, were specified for the Blue Streak machine, which, again, was all about improving combustion. Kawasaki fitted the CDI ignition to the Samurai and Avenger twins for the 1968 model year, by the way.

One feature on the Mach III 500 hints at Kawasaki's uncertainty regarding how well, or otherwise, the bike would be received by older riders, who had grown up with British twins. The 500 was designed to have either a right- or left-foot gear change, with a splined rod emerging from both sides of the crankcases. Kawasaki obviously didn't want to put off Britbike fans keen to 'convert' to Japanese machinery, but habitually used to a right-foot change. The odd habit of having neutral at the bottom of the pattern, with five speeds all reached by shifting up, as seen on the 250/350 twins, remained on the 500.

The chassis betrayed how much development time Kawasaki had put into the engine. A conventional duplex cradle, closely based on the Samurai 250 and featuring thin steel tubing, simply wasn't long enough. Interestingly, the H1 500 has a 55.1in wheelbase – the 250 Samurai features a 55.2in stretch between the wheels. So, Kawasaki made the bigger, more powerful bike shorter – an odd concept.

To steady that lively front end Kawasaki fitted two steering dampers: friction and hydraulic. This 'belt-and-braces' approach around the steering head hints at a certain last minute determination to make the Mach III stay in a reasonably straight line at high speed.

The A1R clubman level road race machine made a big impression on European and American tracks from '67 onwards.

BEFORE THE TRIPLES

The rear of the Mach III chassis received cursory attention; the swingarm and rear shock absorbers on the Mach III look remarkably similar to the items fitted on the Samurai 250. The shocks were noted as being poorly damped in launch reports. The swingarm pivot would also prove an Achilles heel. Manufacturing tolerances could have been better, thus reducing the play inherent in the H1's design. Swingarm bushes were inadequate, also.

Despite this, the Mach III wasn't an especially bad handling machine by the standards of the time. The first generation Honda CB750 from '69 is ponderous and vague, and the T150 Trident tends to 'flop' into slow corners. With hindsight, it's plain that Kawasaki, and other Japanese manufacturers, were not inclined – or perhaps even capable – of mass-producing an excellent chassis in the '60s. A good frame was generally hand-crafted, back in 1968.

Having copied Fontana's brake for the A1-R and A7-R twin cylinder racers, Kawasaki fitted a similar TLS front brake to the Mach III, with Ceriani-esque forks set at a fairly raked-out steering head angle. The aim was stability, but the forks could have been a touch more substantial.

So, by late summer '68, the bike that would be labelled Mach III, H1 and 500 SS was ready for launch across the USA. Having missed the boat with its four-stroke 750 four, beaten to the market by Honda, Kawasaki was no doubt keen to get the fiery triple out there, irrespective of any design flaws.

It was time to light the blue touchpaper and stand well back ...

A super rare model; the American Eagle 350, produced in the late '60s in the USA. Only eight were built; this is believed to be one of four which survive.

CHAPTER TWO

The H1 500 series

Launched in September 1968 in the USA, the H1/Mach III stunned the US motorcycle press with its acceleration over the quarter mile, then the main criteria that many riders used when making a buying decision. Many riders drag raced the H1 in both the USA and Europe, and, compared to rivals like the Honda CB450 and Triumph Daytona 500 twins, the Mach III was in another league – it did exactly what Kawasaki Japan wanted, it trounced the opposition.

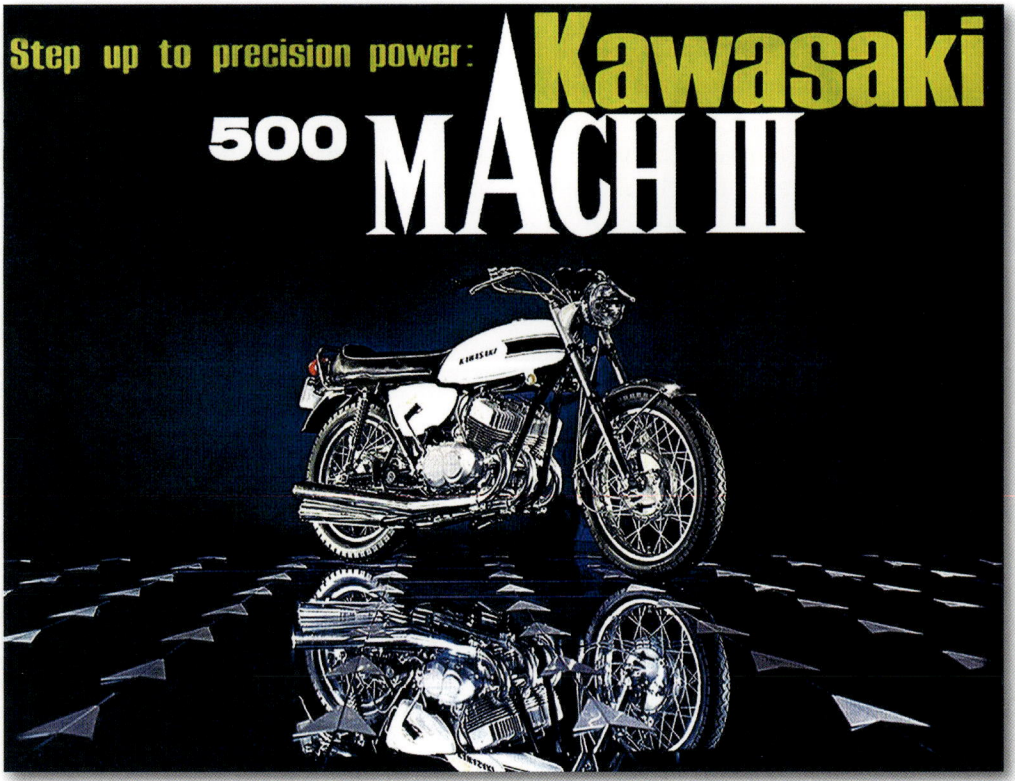

A US market ad for the new Mach III 500 triple.

THE H1 500 SERIES

The 500 H1 also helped put the Kawasaki name on the map for European riders, with its claimed 13 second quarter mile and 110mph top speed. Although the bikes were hard to get hold of in 1969, the H1 quickly became a popular choice in clubman, international, and endurance races in the '69 racing season. Arrival of the H1R race version in late '69 put the Kawasaki name in the blue riband Grand Prix class, too.

The H1 in Europe

The motorcycle market across western Europe was in sharp decline in the late '60s, as an increasing number of people aspired to car ownership, essentially seeing motorcycles as lower class transport; a bit dirty and unreliable. But the Japanese brands had a touch of glamour, and in Britain the 250 and 350 Kawasaki twins had made quite an impression with the enthusiastic younger section of the biking public. The early H1 500 launch reports in the UK press were all from US-based journalists – Brit riders couldn't wait to see this 'fire-breathing' two-stroke triple.

Although Kawasaki was spending large sums setting up a US network in the '60s, it was a different story in Europe. In countries like the UK, Germany, Holland and France, Kawasaki hadn't established individual national import operations, so it was left largely to enterprising dealers to effectively 'launch' the Kawasaki brand in that decade. Detlev Louis started the German operation in Hamburg in the late '60s, Xavier Maugendre began Sidemm in '67, H Floter acquired the Kawasaki import rights in Sweden, and Genoese dealer Marino Abbo began bringing triples into Italy. It was a great opportunity: businessmen could see Kawasaki was a big company, with huge potential, even if Honda, Yamaha and Suzuki had got into Europe first.

"I was one of the first UK Kawasaki dealers," recalls Bill Smith. "I could see the British companies gradually abandoning the small bike market in the late '60s, and the Japanese rescued the situation. Without them, motorcycling would probably have died out in Britain.

"In late '68 I heard that Bridgestone was withdrawing from motorbike manufacturing, which was a shame as they were great bikes. So I wanted another two-stroke franchise. Back then, Read's of London was about the only UK Kawasaki dealer, so I thought I would buy a batch of Kawasaki machines from the factory and sell them in the north-west of England. I think the first order I placed was for a job lot of thirty A1/A7 twins."

The bikes sold well, so Bill thought he would use a trip to Japan to meet Honda as a covert opportunity to learn more about Kawasaki. At the time, Kawasaki was using the London office of Japanese trading company C Itoh & Co as its UK agents, but Bill said nothing and simply turned up at Kawasaki's Kobe factory, politely knocking on the front door. "We had some green tea and what have you," recalls Bill, "then they asked how many ships I wanted to buy – I was in the wrong division! So I found the motorcycle department and they seemed keen to have me as official UK importer, but I had commitments at that time with Honda, so that was impossible. Whilst the factory lines were stopped for lunch I walked through these plastic-covered doors and had a snoop around, eventually stumbling into the R&D department. I saw various two-stroke triples, all kinds of different engine sizes – 250, 350; there was even a 650 – they were obviously planning a range of them. But the most interesting thing was a stripped-down MV Agusta four cylinder racer. I don't quite know how it found its way from European racetracks to Kobe, but that MV probably taught Kawasaki a fair bit about DOHC fours."

The arrival of the H1 in 1969 was very successful for Bill as he recalled some forty years later: "We sold about sixty H1 500s that first year, then about one hundred triples, in all sizes, each year from the Liverpool shop between 1970-73. The H1 wasn't a cheap bike to run, and motorcycling was in a recession in the late '60s, so they were good initial sales volumes. The H1 and

21

THE KAWASAKI TRIPLES BIBLE

A restored 1970 model 500 H1 at the 2009 Classic Mechanics Show.

the smaller triples sold steadily, everything was okay until fuel prices rocketed in '73, but by then Kawasaki was already planning to phase out the two-strokes."

Interestingly, Kawasaki UK's official import figures on the H1 for 1969 are just 23, with 53 quoted for 1970. However, Kawasaki admits that there were "small numbers of private imports" coming in from 1969-74, before Kawasaki Motors UK was set up as a wholly owned subsidiary.

The UK motorcycle press liked the new triple, but was concerned by its voracious thirst for fuel and two-stroke oil. *Motorcyclist Illustrated* reported that a trip to Assen had returned an average 24mpg, with oil consumed at one pint per 100 miles. The UK road testers were also disappointed to discover that the new bike had three sets of points, not the hi-tech, CDI electronic ignition that the US market had, the reason for which was that the CDI ignition caused interference with TV reception, so all European specification H1 models for '69 and '70 came with coils and points.

Elsewhere in Europe, French importer Sidemm – little more than a backstreet shop back then – took small numbers of the H1 in '69, and only in the white colour scheme. Sidemm's Xavier Maugendre believed that having just one colour for each particular model would help potential customers remember the new Kawasaki brand that bit better.

How Xavier Maugendre became the Kawasaki France importer is a story in itself and epitomises the type of entrepreneur who was drawn to the brand. Maugendre was a classically educated young man who studied car and aeronautical engineering,

THE H1 500 SERIES

Left and below: This cutaway H1 500 motor was used to train UK Kawasaki dealership mechanics in the early '70s. It could be plugged into an electrical supply and 'run' slowly in order to see the firing order, port timing, etc.

and then found work at the Citroën R&D facility before joining Volvo France. Later, he switched to Honda motorcycles in the early '60s and worked for the then French Honda import operation. Maugendre thought he could do things better and started the Sidemm operation with just two machines, a W650 and A7 Avenger, just before Christmas 1967. It was a massive gamble and, even more impressively, Maugendre took 100 large capacity bikes from Kawasaki in '68 and sold them, on the road, more or less by himself.

In 1970, Maugendre brought Daniel Baranne, one of the first non-motorcycle industry sponsors, into the sport, and went endurance racing with the H1R: Christian Ravel won on the Sidemm/Baranne machine. Instant publicity resulted: it was that type of go-getting, seat-of-the-pants dealer/importer that Kawasaki usually appointed in Europe, and indeed elsewhere in the early phase of its expansion. As a brand, Kawasaki was in a big hurry.

As regards mainland Europe, Kawasaki had been inviting motorcycle dealers,

THE KAWASAKI TRIPLES BIBLE

wholesalers and shipping agents to Rotterdam since the mid '60s to inspect the latest Kawasaki bikes, which were often sold off the docks in job lots of assorted models. If an importer thought he could sell a particular model, or colour, then they could strike a deal. As Kawasaki had extensive interests in shipping, mining, oil and steel, Holland was the most obvious bridgehead into Europe and the company appointed another typically flamboyant distributor in Holland in the same period.

Dutch courage

Henk Vink, a small-scale importer of mopeds and dealer in NSU cars, was looking for a new brand to import in the late '60s. Ton Pels, Henk's friend and rival in later drag race events, recalls how Henk won the Kawasaki franchise with a spot of canny subterfuge. "Henk and his father had the same Christian name, and there was great rivalry between the two of them. Henk Junior learned that his father was negotiating with Kawasaki to buy bikes straight off one of its ships when it docked in Holland. In the mid '60s, the Japanese company wanted to showcase some of the smaller 175cc and big 650cc twins to dealers. Anyway, Henk telexed Kawasaki that he would agree terms as regards becoming an importer, then hopped on a plane and signed the paperwork.

So, instead of his father, Henk Vink Jr signed for the Kawasaki franchise. Pretty cheeky move, but Kawasaki Japan had no reason to think that this wasn't the Henk Vink it had been dealing with in Holland for some time – so the deal stood."

The ruse worked and the young Henk began selling the 125cc Kawasaki trial bike, the 175cc commuter, and then, later, the Samurai and Avenger twins. Ton remembers that Henk went drag racing purely to publicise the speed of the twins and later triple cylinder bikes.

"Sure he wanted to win, but really it was for fun and to raise the profile of the Kawasaki brand. He raced the twins using a mechanic

Both Europe and the USA were allocated the 500 triple and 250/350 twins in the '69 model year. Europe did not receive the SS (Street Scrambler) 250/350 variants, however.

24

THE H1 500 SERIES

from New Zealand, I think, then when the 500 H1 came out he started working with Jan Smit. It was really successful and, of course, Henk went on to race the 750 H2 machines, then the Z1 fours in the '70s."

Like Sidemm in France, Reads of London, or Marino Abbo in Italy, Vink was a Kawasaki importer who liked to prove the worth of the Kawasaki brand via competition. The great thing about all that glory-chasing from Kawasaki Japan's point of view was that it spent just a fraction of the true cost of going racing, since the importers did most of the work and ran teams for the company. It was a brilliant low budget strategy, but in the USA the philosophy was different.

There, Kawasaki offered huge sums in contingency prize funds and let the first Kawasaki rider past the flag take it all. It then extensively publicised any kind of speed record, race win, drag race time or anything else that built the performance reputation of the big K. The spending involved in backing the launch of the H1 and the H1R, when compared to Europe, was enormous. It was make or break for the brand on the H1 – and Kawasaki knew it.

H1 USA

Selling the quarter mile pounder

Over in the USA, marketing of the first Kawasaki triple, called the Mach III, was a totally different ball game from the patchy distribution in Europe. Kawasaki had been in the US market for almost a decade, rapidly building a dealer network and establishing offices on both seaboards, plus Chicago.

Some of the last minute development work, including styling of the fuel tank and side panels, was completed by the American office in Santa Ana, California. The Mach III name tag was added by the US marketing department, too, after it rejected the H1 model name as too boring. There was a call for the bike to be named Blue Streak, after the codename for the entire project, but Mach III won the day. A few journalists were flown to Japan to test the pre-production prototypes, plus project 'Blue Streak' was

tested extensively in California, before official launch to the motorcycle press.

Kawasaki dealer rep Ed Moran recalls those days: "I was the service manager for the east coast (east of the Mississippi River), plus some mid-west states in '68. I was sent to Santa Ana to help test and evaluate pre-production, H1/Mach III models. I think there were three actual bikes.

"We did some riding around southern California and also some drag racing, I believe, at Carlsbad. Jim Thorpe, Tony Nicosia and myself hammered them up the strip. We did many low 12 second runs, but not sure if we got into the 11s. I do recall that I put one at 11.9 at a later date."

Ed then had a bit of a marketing

Today's 500 triple owners will be amazed to learn that the bike "handles great" and has sparkplugs that "don't have to be gapped."

25

THE KAWASAKI TRIPLES BIBLE

brainwave. "Anyway I was so impressed with the performance I presented the idea to Kawasaki that we bring a brand new Mach III to a drag race, open the crate, take the bike out, put oil and gas in it – then race it. I seemed to have more confidence that it could be done than anyone else at the time."

His strategy worked: when the Mach III was launched to the US motorcycle press, this was more or less what happened, with demo runs taking place before the journalists were allowed to have a go. The quarter mile time was a crucial selling tool then, and an entire ad campaign was built around the new Kawasaki's astonishing performance on the strip. Journalists were wowed by the Mach III's performance 'straight from the crate.'

Motorcycle magazines lost no time in running features on tuning the 500 Mach III for even better acceleration, and later, sharpening handling. It also impressed the American bike public with its toughness; it could be run hard up the strip stone cold, would set fast times, and yet very rarely seize up.

Ed Moran recalls that the engine was really tough by the standards of the day, though its Achilles heel was the electrics. "At one point early during testing Varsol [a paint thinner] was put into the gas tank by mistake, The bike ran but knocked like hell. For me, that was testimony to the reliability of the thing, though later on we did have trouble with the CDI units on the Mach III."

Solving the problem involved the expertise of one of Kawasaki's many sub-contractor suppliers, "In '69 I travelled to dealers around the country with an engineer from Mitsubishi, purely because of the CDI failures. It was a wonderful experience for me as I learnt so much.

Below, left: In 1970, Kawasaki made much of the CDI unit as an advanced feature on the 500 model.

Below, right: A tie-in with the Revell model kit company was another chance for Kawasaki to promote the 500 Mach III. The overall winner received a new H1A, Bell helmet, and Kawasaki team jacket.

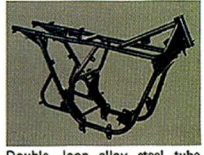

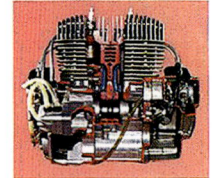

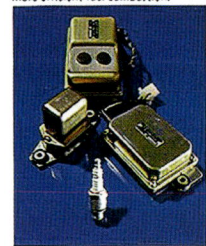

The H1 500 Series

I could take the 'A' box apart, diagnose it, then take parts from another one and make a good CDI box. I paid close attention to that engineer!"

Kawasaki also placed a large number of advertisements in the US motorcycle press, plus offered machines as competition prizes as part of the marketing push. Kawasaki USA's agency originated a radio advert which proclaimed the H1 to be "The fastest production motorcycle in the world," and also set up a lucrative prize fund for those who fancied having a crack at the '69 Daytona 200 and other road races. Kawasaki also emulated other motorcycle and scooter manufacturers by placing the 500 in movies and TV shows. The publicity machine was full throttle for the Mach III.

The reaction from US journalists was almost universal praise. *Cycle* magazine liked the metered oil injection to the main bearings, with back-up oil splash feed via the inlet ports, plus the CDI ignition was hailed as 'space age' technology, which it was when compared to the contact breaker points then fitted to most bikes.

Another feature that all the US magazines loved was that the bike retailed for $999, or $400 less than the recently launched Honda CB750 Four. The Kawasaki was lauded as well made, and, despite lacking an electric starter or front disc brake, many journalists thought that, of the two, it was the better value Superbike.

The '70 season saw the Peacock Grey colour option offered in all markets, along with a new Candy Red scheme. The oil tank side panel now had the words 'Electronic ignition' set on it. The '70 model year H1/Mach III was the same as the '69 model in all other respects.

However, about halfway through the year, Kawasaki began shipping H1/Mach III models with a revised CDI cover on the right-hand side of the engine. Owners of the original '69 Mach III had complained that water was getting into the electrics, and so a larger cover was fitted with an extra plastic sleeve for the wiring. The new oil pump and ignition assembly was fitted from engine number 8800. The rotor shaft became a QD item after this number, too. Finally, the oil pump cover got a little drain grommet and a new distributor gasket from engine number 11300, according to Kawasaki servicing records.

Other faults on early H1s include having incorrect Champion L-19V sparkplugs,

Above, left: The ad spend, plus the sheer performance of the triple, guaranteed Kawasaki would feature on quite a few front covers of the US motorcycle press in '69.

Above, right: The 1970 Japan spec 500SS/Mach III was available in Candy Red.

The Kawasaki Triples Bible

later H1s had UL-19Vs. Some L-19V plugs went into early H2 models, too, by the way. Engine numbers up to KAE03138 on the 500 H1 series made do with 6mm studs on the exhaust header pipe mounts, but after that a stepped 6mm-8mm stud was used for greater strength. You can't do a retro fit, according to the Kawasaki tech bulletin.

1969-70 500 H1 – Mach III – 500SS spotter's guide

Drum front brake, lightning bolt graphic on side panel.
Colours were midnight white, peacock grey.
Stainless steel front mudguard.
Rear brake had a sliding vent on backing plate.
The H1/Mach III had Champion UL-19V sparkplugs from new.
OE tyres were Dunlop Gold Seals, 19 inch front, 18 inch rear.
Late '70 model H1 had a bigger CDI cover, Candy Red colour in Europe and Japan; Peacock Grey in USA. (This shade looks almost black).
Some US-spec '70 models had knee pads with an indented 'Kawasaki' logo set into the rubber pad.
Engine numbers: KAE 00001 on.
Frame numbers: KAF 00001 on.

500 H1 – MACH III – 500SS collector's notes

The vast majority of production was exported to the USA. Accurate numbers are 'not available' from Kawasaki, but sales of around 4000 units in '69, followed by 12,000-14,000 in '70, are estimated. The H1 didn't go on sale until March of '69, so it was a short model year.
Numbers sold into Europe are impossible to gauge accurately, but a rough guess would be around 700 '69 models registered, arriving from about June. Maybe 1000 examples of the H1 '70 model were sold. The first '69 H1 is likely to be the most collectable out of a diminishing pool of survivors.

Jim Breslin worked for the Canadian Kawasaki distributor, F Manley Corporation, and later for Kawasaki Canada. He estimates that "the Canadian market was approximately a tenth of the USA market." so we can estimate that around 1500-1700 500 Mach III bikes sold during '69 and '70.
If you import a US-spec '69 or '70 Mach III to Europe there's a danger that the original CDI can damage a variety of modern electronic devices placed within close range, such as digital video cameras, mobile phones, etc.

500 HIA 1971

Softening the edges

Apart from colour changes and a new shape gas tank boasting 'laser line' decals, which also lost the '60s-style knee cut-outs, the H1A was largely unchanged from its predecessor. There had been some port work inside the motor; essentially, the bridges had been removed from the intake ports to improve gas flow. According to road test data at the time, this didn't make the H1A any faster over the quarter mile, and those who loved ripping off standing quarters all day long might have had chain problems. The original DID drive chain was replaced with a heavy duty EK chain from August '71. The new chain needs the guard to be moved slightly to stop it fouling, by the way.

There were also modifications to the CDI ignition, which US service manager Ed Moran and his associate from Mitsubishi helped diagnose on the first generation Mach III.

Shocks and fork internals received a few tweaks, as some US journalists had complained the ride was too harsh during the '69 launch, but handling remained fairly marginal at high speed.

If anything, the marketing push behind the bike intensified in the USA. Eight class speed records were taken by the 500 Mach III at Bonneville in late '70, and the top Kawasaki USA dealers had been flown to Tahiti in the autumn to see the '71 model

THE H1 500 SERIES

H1A in Candy Blue, the only officially listed colour scheme for the model year.

line-up. The contingency money offered for race winners on the H1R was huge, and dealer-racers like New Jersey-based Ed Moran had no doubt that the resulting publicity helped sell the bikes. "I would win a race and it made the local papers – I used to give away T-shirts with my name on 'em. The interest that year was huge."

The massive Kawasaki motorcycle press ad campaign continued throughout '71, as Kawasaki planned the launch of the 'Tri-Stars' for the following year, with the 750 and 350 on schedule to join the 500 in late '71. The US retail price rose by around $25 for the '71 model year H1A 500; the Tahiti trip had to be paid for somehow, presumably …

1971 H1A spotter's guide
The only factory colour was Candy Blue.
The 'Kawasaki' and '500' were laser-cut decals, not painted on.
Different shape gas tank, no knee cut-outs.

Engine numbers: KAE 21876 on.
Frame numbers: KAF 23626 on.

H1A collector's notes
In Europe there was an attempt to push the bike harder, but key markets still lacked comprehensive distributor networks. Official UK sales figures for the H1A model were just 280 units; Sidemm in France probably sold around twice that number. The H1A remained an expensive bike in Europe compared to its bargain US price.

European riders were taking notice of the H1, as the H1R race machine had an excellent GP debut season, and '71 brought Kawasaki its first 500cc class GP victory in Spain. Total European sales volumes can be estimated at between 2500 and 3000 units for '71.

Again, the vast majority of sales for the H1A were in North America. Ed Moran recalls that, in '71, he was the second most successful dealer in the USA, selling exactly 488 triples, mainly 500s, as the 350 and 750 arrived very late in the year. Total US and Canadian sales were probably around 12,000-14,000 units.

The Kawasaki Triples Bible

This heavily modified H1A is on display in the Musee de Moto in Marseilles.

The '71 US market Kawasaki line-up.

H1B 1972

Superstar Tri-Star

1972 was a huge year for Kawasaki, as late summer of '71 saw the first 350 Mach II arrive, and November was the press launch for the 74bhp 750 Mach IV. There were rave reviews from the US motorcycle press for the new machines, especially the 750, and the 500 formed part of the famous 'Year of the Tri-Stars' ad campaign which featured riders wearing space suits; well, okay, white overalls – and pulling a triple-row wheelie in the brochures and magazine ads.

The 500 Mach III, known as the H1B in Europe, was given a thorough makeover to help it fit into the new line-up. Most obvious changes were the disc brake at the front (with mountings on the fork leg for a second disc), Candy Orange paintwork, and shorter front fender, now painted rather than chromed. Paintwork and decals were

The H1 500 Series

designed by Molly of California, incidentally, with candy colours mixed in the USA and the paint formula passed to the factory in Japan.

The other news was that Kawasaki decided to revert to points and coil ignition on the '72 H1B. *Cycle Guide* reckoned the reason was cost-cutting, but noted that the bike ran just as well without the hi-tech CDI unit. Sparkplugs changed to NGK BH9s. Later in '72, a dealer service bulletin advised that points were set at 20 degrees BTDC, as the points had a tendency to move with wear and tear, and the original factory setting of 23 degrees didn't allow much margin for slippage. The result was that some early H1Bs suffered detonation and holed pistons. Kawasaki was still on a steep learning curve with the triples at this stage.

Cycle Guide magazine discovered why its test machine wobbled above 80mph – the wheels were out of alignment by half an inch. The '72 Mach III had new front forks made from aluminium, with revised internals, plus a new steering damper was fitted just below the gas tank to backup the centrally-mounted damper on the headstock. The new damper was subject to a factory recall later in '72 to prevent flexing when set at its stiffest position: a new bracket was installed from March '72.

At the back end the H1B received tapered rear wheel spokes, thicker by about half a millimetre as they join the wheel rim. Another minor but welcome tweak was a more secure welded fastening on the gear lever, to prevent it working loose and suffering 'play.'

The Mach III, US-spec 500 also had wider set indicators front and rear to meet new regulations that demanded winkers be spaced further from the machine's central bodywork to make them stand out more. The stalks that the indicators are set onto are liable to let them droop a little – it's a normal feature, noted in contemporary road tests of the time.

The new '72 model was heavier than the older 500, so efforts were made to improve performance. The airbox was redesigned, with a new filter element and different inlet tracts to the carbs. Early models were missing an 'air silencer' in the airbox, which may have been deliberate to retain the performance edge on the bikes road tested by magazines. Whatever the case, the air silencer was retro-fitted as a service upgrade item, then a new air cleaner, plus revised carb settings applied from engine number KAE61607. Main jets changed from 100 to 95, and needle jets from 0-4 to 0-4.8mm; throttle valve cutaway dropped from 2.5 to 2.0; pilot jet remained at 30.

The same four cable system connected the throttle to the 28mm Mikuni carbs, and the oil pump, making it easy for the bike to go 'off song,' especially when matched to three sets of contact breaker points. The early H1 models could smoke from the right-hand cylinder, and a new oil pump end cover and O-ring kit was specified from October '72 production. According to Kawasaki, this was offered as a conversion kit on older H1 models.

Compression rose slightly from 6.8:1 to 7:1 on the H1B, and new exhausts were claimed to improve overall engine breathing – and fuel economy. *Cycle Guide* recorded a shocking 12mpg on a high speed test, so maybe the H1B was breathing a little too heavily ...

'70s Tri-Star advert.

The Kawasaki Triples Bible

Whatever the true power output of the H1B (Kawasaki still claimed 60bhp) the quarter mile and top speed tests showed it was slowing, the main reasons for which were heavier baffled exhausts to meet stricter noise, and emissions regulations in the USA, plus an increase in dry weight by some 25lb. The best quarter mile time *Supercycle* could get for the '72 Mach III was 12.9 seconds: the original Mach III from '69 had a best of 12.4, a big difference. Top speed had dropped from 122 to 112mph.

The HIB was overshadowed by the arrival of the new H2 750 in the USA and Canada, but remained a top-selling machine, despite its slightly diminished performance. *Motorcycle World* noted that in a head-to-head test against Honda's new CB500 four, the Kawasaki utterly trashed the Honda over the quarter mile with a 12.8 second time, whilst the leisurely Honda could manage only a 14.6 second best run. The magazine also noted that the Kawasaki smoked plentifully, and wondered if the injectolube oil system was set to deliver an excess of oil to play safe?

The bottom line, as they say in the USA, was that the Kawasaki still cost around $1000 to buy, whereas the rival CB500 was $400 more. This discrepancy helped the '72 model achieve excellent sales figures in both the USA and Canada during the year.

Smoking across europe

The arrival of the '72 range of triples helped Kawasaki make great progress in Europe and Australia. The 750 joined the Superbike club alongside the Triumph Trident, Norton Commando, Honda CB750, and Suzuki's new GT750. The Suzuki was a two-stroke, but no match for the Kawasaki with a softer, more touring-orientated power delivery. The smaller 350 and 250 triples also brought Kawasaki a whole raft of teenage customers, looking for their first 'real' motorcycle.

The 500 H1B formed part of the restyled line-up for '72 and Sidemm in France, Agrati UK, and Henk Vink in Holland all sold more triples as the brand expanded its reach. In Germany, Detlev Louis had been importing the Kawasaki brand via his dealership in Hamburg since the launch of the 500H1. By '72, a West German dealer network was well established, and the H1B/Mach III was a steady seller that year. At that time, Germany, like many other European countries, had archaic licencing laws which allowed a young rider to pass a basic riding test on a 125 or 250cc machine, then ride anything they could afford.

In France, Sidemm was reaping the benefits of starting the Moto Revue Coupe Kawasaki series, with a smaller 250 class joining the 350 S2s on track. The 500 sold very well that year in France alongside the new 750, and Sidemm's Xavier Maugendre also put the bigger triples into a chase sequence of a French cop thriller movie. Placing the bikes there to maximum advantage was helped by the fact that it was Maugendre's brother who produced the movie.

In the UK, the situation was improved, but not much. Agrati Sales refused to loan test bikes to top-selling titles like *Bike* magazine, and couldn't be bothered sending photographs of '72 and '73 models to *Motorcycle Mechanics* when it put together an Earls Court Show feature. Despite the haphazard efforts of Agrati, which resulted in relatively low publicity across the UK motorcycle press, some 180 H1B models sold that year, according to Agrati's own figures.

A German brochure for the Mach III/H1B '72 model. Note the orange and red side reflectors, similar to US models. "The fastest 500cc motorcycle," claims the copy.

The H1 500 Series

Buy it Saturday, race on Sunday

Drag racing the H1 was popular in Europe as well as the USA, it was just less publicised by Kawasaki themselves, who were concentrating their resources on the US market. It was a relatively cheap form of motorcycle sport in the 70s, with low entry fees and plenty of run-wot-u-brung classes.

Phil Steele bought a '72 model H1B in 1974 and took it to Santa Pod raceway just for a laugh. He has been hooked on drag racing and sprints ever since, but can still recall those first runs down the quarter mile;

"I went along with a mate to the Spring Nationals in '74, April 14th-15th it was, I'll never forget it. The H1B was an absolutely stock machine except for Read Titan rear sets. The photo was taken early in the day and I remember racing Mick Carter who was on a

Left and above: Engine and instrument details on the UK-spec '72 H1B 500.

The Kawasaki Triples Bible

Phil at his first drag race on his '72 H1B machine. Totally stock. Best time at the meeting was 13.6 seconds.

By late '75 Phil was getting into the 12s with Campbell expansions and a Flak tune on the head and barrels. Note the mudflap and fork gaiters – Phil used the bike on the road, so wanted it to be practical.

Commando, in the Street Legal class. I ran a 13.6 second time, but Mick knocked me out with a 13.2 seconds time. I was gutted, but determined to come back for more."

Phil recalls that it took a few seasons before he got into the 12s with the triple and the bike needed modifying to achieve that. "The first thing I had done was a Brian Flak tune," says Phil. "He was the man then and he'd started drag racing Norton twins, I think, before switching to Kawasaki. It cost what seemed like a fortune at the time, about 30 quid, or a week's wages! Skimmed heads, ports matched up, chamfered and opened up a bit.

"I then had Campbell Geometrics make up a set of expansion pipes for it. Ran K&N filters, too. Campbell's sold the pipes as a kit and you had to weld the sections yourself. You could run in the Street class with the pipes on. I was getting a top end of about 105, 106mph terminal and low 13s, then high 12s."

By '76, the H1B, even with its tweaked engine, was struggling against supercharged twins, or tuned four-stroke Z1s.

"It was hard to squeeze anymore from it really," continued Phil. "We all read the drag race mags from the States and I lowered the H1, dropped the forks in yokes, ran low rear tyre pressures, and tried a wider Avon tyre as well. By that time there were guys running the 750 H2 in the Street Legal class, too. It was a reliable bike, I maybe took the clutch apart a few times, but no trouble from the bottom end, or gearbox, and it never seized."

Phil remembers that he nearly flipped the bike a few times, so fitted wheelie bars. He used to spend a long time setting the ignition timing before each meeting. Later in the bike's race career it was sponsored by a local pub, and so became a Team Kings Arms Kawasaki machine. It was sold, as a road legal bike with stock pipes, a custom two-tone green paintwork, back in 1977.

1972 H1B spotter's notes
Distinctive swoopy decals on tank.
Only available in Pearl Candy Orange.
USA, Canada, Japan and German market models all had side reflectors.
Mudguard painted orange, not chrome.
OE sparkplugs changed to NGK from Champion.
Engine numbers: KAE 54101 on.
Frame numbers: KAF 48763 on.

1972 H1B collector's notes
The vast majority of H1B models were sold in the USA and Canada; a reasonable guess would be in the 10-12,000 units bracket. European sales expanded quite dramatically in '72, but the H1B still probably sold under 2000 units across western Europe.
Many restored H1B models in Europe today have been imported from the 'sunbelt' states of the USA, where the bikes weren't subjected to wet roads, and so rust far less. Many machines with local, and age-related, registration plates may well be from North America. There are also amalgamations of H1A/B/C models, usually later engines set inside earlier frames.
Some classic motorcycle experts reckon that Kawasaki triples can run badly today because of botched 'tuning' by the owners. That undoubtedly happened, especially

The H1 500 Series

to early triples in the USA, where magazines ran features showing how to file the ports in the motor, fit aftermarket pipes, etc. But it is also worth noting that for the H1B model Kawasaki itself issued several pieces of incorrect information in dealer workshop manuals. For example, the wrong wiring diagram for the HIB alternator was printed. In summer '72, a service manual was sent out to all dealers containing no information at all for the H1B. So, it's worth bearing in mind that a dealer-serviced machine from that era may well have been partially sabotaged by Kawasaki.

1972 H1C collector's notes

According to Kawasaki Japan, the H1C model 500 triple from 1972 doesn't exist. But, according to UK triples aficionado Rick Brett, some 1800 examples of the H1C were produced and mainly sold in the US market.

The H1C was a curious machine, which had the entire front end and engine from the H1A model, plus exhausts, and was then dressed in the orange colours and new gas tank of the H1B. It appears it was a kind of stopgap model for the US market, and a few US road tests of '72 list CDI ignition, plus the old, lighter dry weight figure in the tech spec, yet the main text deals with Kawasaki's backward move to contact breaker points ignition.

As far as the author can research, no H1C models were officially imported to Europe, ostensibly because it had the CDI ignition which interfered with TV and radio reception. But as Kawasaki refuses to acknowledge that the model ever existed, information is scant.

What is certain is that many H1C models were imported to Europe in the '90s, as the classic bike boom swept US dealerships, farms and warehouses clean of older and almost every complete H1 that was for sale. Older imported bikes are generally allocated age-related registration plates, so a later import can appear to be a European H1C.

Pete Amson from DK motorcycles in Staffordshire, England, recalls: "At one stage in the '90s we had a room full of triples. We were bringing container loads of bikes across every month from the States, they were so cheap. Now people are asking as much for an original H1 airbox as we paid per machine back then."

The unofficial H1C model which Kawasaki doesn't like to mention ... (Courtesy Rick Brett)

1973 H1D

Greenie, but not so meanie

For the '73 model year Kawasaki gave the 500 triple an extensive makeover, but decided to style the bike differently from its 750 H2 big brother and smaller sized 350 S2 and 250 S1. We can only speculate that Kawasaki was so wrapped up launching the Z1 900 in late '72, designing a range of four-strokes, racing the H2R, and laying plans for its own European distributor operation, that the 'family' styling theme was forgotten on the H1D.

The H1D, in many ways, was a better machine than its predecessors. It certainly looked the part, and featured a Candy Lime Green paint scheme which suited the bike

35

The Kawasaki Triples Bible

H-1 500

Candy Lime Green was the only official colour for the '73 H1D, but it is possible some early H1E two-tone paint schemes appeared on late '73 registered H1D models.

perfectly. CDI ignition made a comeback, and this time it was a more advanced unit, as fitted to the H2A 750, which didn't send 'white snow' across the TV sets of Europe. The new seat and tailpiece improved the looks and the grab rail replaced the old seat strap.

Apart from styling updates, there were serious attempts to make the bike handle better and return more mpg. The frame featured new engine mounts, plus the swing arm was lengthened by half an inch, and the forks kicked out by another degree to steady the steering. Kawasaki felt confident enough to do away with the friction steering damper mounted on the headstock, retaining just the hydraulic one on the side. The reality was, however, that the bike still handled a touch unpredictably.

Inside the engine the oil pump received a new gasket tweak from engine number KAE83625 to help prevent the banjo bolts on the locking plate from working loose. There was also a service notice to dealers instructing them to very carefully feed the oil tank vent pipe down the left side of the bike to avoid pinching. There had been reports of blocked vent pipes causing oil pump starvation – followed by seizure, obviously.

The gear change mechanism had a shim kit added from engine number KAE59017, well into the '73 H1D production run. This was to combat the old bugbear of missing gears when quickshifting, and the shims were placed in the gear dogs. Sometimes the gears themselves just didn't quite line up correctly inside the 'box from new. The old saying that "just because it's factory made doesn't mean it works" is always true with '70s motorcycles, which is why so many racers blueprinted their engines back then.

The H1 500 Series

According to contemporary road tests the H1D wasn't great in the twisty stuff; *Cycle* reported that the bike simply weaved and wiggled its way through corners. The new shocks were generally considered too soft, and ground clearance was still poor, with both side and centre stands decking (touching the ground through corners) too easily. As a plus point it did have a bigger, 11.5 inch front disc brake, which meant it was possible to brake harder before pogo-ing around the next corner, for example.

Once again, Kawasaki changed the exhausts to make the bike quieter and less greedy on fuel. The dry weight of the bike went up slightly, and this, coupled with changes to the carburettors, officially robbed the H1D of 1bhp – now at a claimed 59bhp, developed at 8000rpm. The reality was that the H1D had lost about half a second off its quarter mile times, and fuel consumption had improved from an abysmal 18-20mpg to a still gas-guzzling 23-25mpg.

In terms of making the 500 more practical, Kawasaki partially succeeded, but had knocked the edge off performance and effectively begun to kill off the model's very reason for being: dodgy handling wasn't really an issue for potential buyers, but, for many Kawasaki 500 fans, slower acceleration certainly took the shine off the H1D.

1973 H1D spotter's guide
US-spec H1Ds have no seat strap, Euro models have.
Two-tone Candy Lime Green paintwork was the only colour scheme.
New oil pump/CDI unit housing gives crankcases a lumpy profile.
US models have Mach III in small letters on side panels.
Sight glass located within oil tank.
Flatter handlebars on some European spec models.
New instrument cluster with central console.
Engine numbers: KAE 00000 on.
Frame numbers: H1F 00001 on.

1973 H1D collector's notes
In the USA it seems the H1E colour scheme, or the actual H1E, might have arrived by the summer of '73. Certainly road test bikes featuring the '74 paintwork can be seen in '73 editions – but were these prototypes for press/trade evaluation? Whether these were the first H1E bikes in volume, hitting the US market, is a moot point. A guesstimate on USA and Canada sales on the H1D would be around 9000 units.

In the UK Agrati Sales received notice in '73 that its contract was to be terminated in '74, so officially just 20 H1D models made it to UK dealers. There is a possibility that some UK Kawasaki dealers sourced stock directly from Japan, or mainland Europe, but numbers were probably small as petrol was actually rationed during late '73 across the UK, so 25mpg motorcycles weren't in great demand.

Overall in Europe, the new Z1 received the largest share of Kawasaki's marketing budget. It was named "Machine of The Year" by almost every motorcycle magazine in Western Europe. The larger 500 and 750 triples sold especially well in France, Germany, Italy and Scandinavia, although demand definitely fell off after the oil blockade late in '73.

An educated guess of units sold for the H1D would be around 2800 '73 across Europe. Again, there are no reliable figures worth quoting.

1974 H1E

For whom the bell tolls
It was obvious by '74 that the party was over for two-stroke motorcycles, especially large capacity engine models. Both the EPA in the US and European governments were busy drafting laws that would effectively render the old 'smokers' illegal. Manufacturers were given emissions and noise targets well in advance of the legislation penned in for most developed economies.

It was no surprise to find that the '74 H1E had yet more work carried out to its engine, in order to make sure less unburnt fuel escaped from its exhausts. To achieve this, Kawasaki returned to the 19th century and added check valves in the bottom end of the engine. Joseph Day pioneered the use of check valves in his two-stroke motor of 1891, and Kawasaki used them on the H2 series from its '71 inception.

The beauty of a check valve is its simplicity; you can vary crankcase pressure at a given point of the engine's cycle – like

The Kawasaki Triples Bible

the valves in a human heart, all you're really doing is moderating flow by creating a tiny vacuum. So the H1E's check valves helped deliver extra oil to the main bearings, but this was not to deal with any oil starvation problems – the H1 500 has a tough bottom end – but rather to ensure less oil-rich vapour made its way up from the crankcase to the combustion chamber, since a two-stroke runs as a kind of constant fuel/air pump, or doesn't work at all.

New two-tone Candy Lime Green, or Candy Red, were the official colour schemes for '74.

This H1E is a US-spec bike, imported to the UK in the late '80s.

So, we can guess that Kawasaki thought the H1E would be more likely to meet emissions targets, thanks to the check valves, but, with hindsight, can see that the attempt was pretty much doomed to fail as the two-stroke engine was on its way out, at least as far as the USA was concerned.

What other improvements did the H1E definitely have? Well, there was another frame re-jig with the wheelbase now stretched out to 56.5 inches, an inch longer than the H1D. The engine was rubber-mounted to reduce vibration at higher rpm, and a new CDI unit was claimed to extend plug life and low rpm response.

The H1E received a gearbox tweak as

THE H1 500 SERIES

This H1E has black plug caps, but, for some markets, these were metal alloy.

well; the early H1 series reported problems with third gear engagement, so from engine number KAE087023, Kawasaki tried to resolve the problem by widening the base of the shift fork from 21.0mm to 24.5mm, with the objective of keeping the fork more rigid on the shift drum. (The H2 model in '74 had the same mod, by the way.) The H1E still came with three spare plugs under the seat, of course, and Kawasaki also added a ground/earthing wire halfway through the production run to combat reports of the bike misfiring, apparently due to the engine moving on its rubber mountings.

Contemporary road tests logged the ageing triple's painful demise. *Bike* magazine in the UK recorded a leisurely 14.02 second quarter mile time. US testers found the bike could still run in the mid 13 second bracket, but was a far cry from brochure claims of 12.4 seconds for the H1E. *Bike* also noted that handling on the E model was still a touch challenging and fuel consumption a scary 23mpg average. The H1E was a slower, less explosive, triple than the D model, which was already sanitised compared the original H1. But worse was to come ...

1974 H1E spotter's guide
US-spec models had raised handlebars, side reflectors.
Brake wear indicator on the rear drum.
19 inch front, 18 inch rear wheel sizes, Dunlop OE fitment.
UK-spec bikes had seat straps, US models grab rail only.
Front mudguard is chrome, not painted.
New smaller CDI unit, same large crankcase cover.
UK-spec models came with twin mirrors as OE fitment.
Engine numbers: KAE 87001 on.
Frame numbers: H1F 17001 on.

39

THE KAWASAKI TRIPLES BIBLE

H1E collector's notes

Kawasaki UK was set up in autumn '74 and claims some 200 H1E models were imported to the UK market that year. France, Italy and Germany enjoyed good sales of the 500 H1E, despite the fuel crisis. A guesstimate on European sales for the H1E would be around 3500 units in total. Kawasaki was busily setting up wholly owned European distributors during '74-75, so marketing stepped up a gear as a result.

Once again North America absorbed the majority of H1E production. A reasonable estimate would be around 10,000 units sold in the USA and Canada. Other significant markets included Japan, Australia, and South Africa.

1975 H1F

Clean but not sober

The H1F is perhaps one of the least loved Kawasaki triples. The company had little choice but to detune the model for '75, as the state of California – where a large proportion of triples were sold – continued along the path of cleaner air and reduced noise.

For '75, the H1F had a restrictor tract placed on top of its airbox, which helped minimise induction 'moan,' and obviously reduced overall gas flow efficiency. The

An unrestored H1F on show at Stafford on the Kawasaki Triples UK Club stand in 2009, in the rare, USA-spec brown colour scheme.

restrictor was shaped like the plastic wee bottle usually found next to a hospital bed and faced backwards, so air had to flow around 180 degrees to get into the airbox.

Less air in, especially when the throttle is cracked open suddenly, usually means less power. *Cycle Guide* dyno-tested a H1F and found just 43bhp at the rear wheel. Kawasaki was still claiming peak output of 59bhp at 8000rpm – the same as the model's predecessor – but it is difficult to believe that the airbox changes didn't chop off a few bhp.

Cycle Guide noted that the H1F on test had "three different shades of brown" in its paintwork, suggesting Kawasaki was switching attention to the four-stroke street bike range by '75. The brown colour wasn't offered for the European market, by the way. Clutch slip was so bad that Kawasaki had to replace it during the test and the bike was out of tune after 2500 miles on the clock. That said, it is remarkable that a best quarter mile time of 13.26 was recorded, almost a second quicker than that which UK magazine *Bike* recorded for the H1D. Maybe there was a Nebraskan tailwind …

The retail price of the bike had risen to around $1500 by now, and Kawasaki's best-selling model in '75 was the humble Z400 twin. A dull plodder maybe, but capable of returning over 50mpg – which mattered, even in America. Most riders must have thought the H1 had reached the end of the line, which it had, but Kawasaki threw one final roll of the dice; the 52bhp KH500, which is covered in the KH series chapters of this book.

1975 H1F spotter's guide

Brown colour scheme fairly rare, offered for North American market only.
Usual high 'bars, reflectors on forks and top of shocks.
No 'Mach III' lettering on side panels.
Central decal on fuel tank has 'pointy' front, rather than rounded off.
No grab strap on US-spec models, still on European H1Fs.
Chromed front mudguard, not painted.
Engine number: KAE102400.
Frame number: H1F32400.

1975 H1F collector's notes

The brown painted models, rather than the more common Candy Sky Blue, or Candy Green, are likely to be more collectable, simply due to their scarcity. The H1F model was the last of the 500s to retain the neutral position in the gearbox at the bottom of the shift pattern. If it has a one-down, four-up pattern, it's a KH500 engine in an earlier H1 chassis.

Kawasaki UK has no available figures for 1975, but marketing at that time was squarely aimed at the smaller 250/400 triples and the new four-strokes. It seems unlikely that more than 500 H1F models arrived in the UK that year. It's worth noting that, by the mid '70s, some UK forces personnel bought 500s in West Germany, as a favourable tax perk allowed them to save on the full price. Very few of those motorcycles remained in Germany as most were shipped out with their owners.

The H1F sold well in Italy, as Kawasaki Italia had been set up the year previously and the 500 H1R had enjoyed some success in the national championship and the famous Imola 200 race in previous years. Some Italian enthusiasts reckon that many of the later H1 500 models were bought up by collectors from northern Europe during the '80s and early '90s, as rust claimed many of the last of the locally registered H1 models.

CHAPTER THREE

KH500

By '76 Kawasaki was very much concentrating on its newer four-stroke models in the US market.

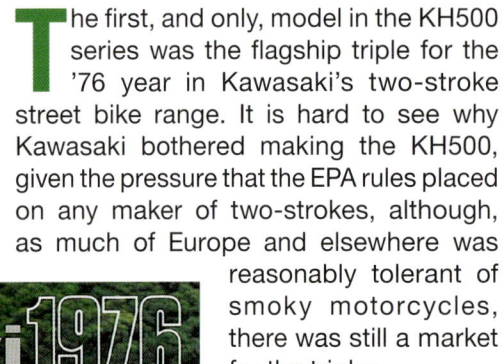

The first, and only, model in the KH500 series was the flagship triple for the '76 year in Kawasaki's two-stroke street bike range. It is hard to see why Kawasaki bothered making the KH500, given the pressure that the EPA rules placed on any maker of two-strokes, although, as much of Europe and elsewhere was reasonably tolerant of smoky motorcycles, there was still a market for the triples.

Kawasaki gave the triples a really thorough update for '76. All remaining bikes had new electrical systems, but the KH500 also had a better headlight (same as the '76 Z1); the paintwork changed, of course, plus the suspension was tweaked, it got a new front wheel, a kill switch added, and the seat altered. The main jets dropped from 92.5 on the H1E/F series to 75 on the KH500 as part of the overall detuning process.

Goodbye green meanie

The KH500 was morphing into something of a sports-tourer, although the concept hadn't really been invented back then. Rivals like Suzuki's GT550 triple and the Honda CB500 four were especially popular in the USA then, and, as American riders were keen on travelling vast distances, the KH500 became a more laidback machine. Features such as the less prominent 'paddles' on the handlebar grips showed that Kawasaki was looking for older, more mature customers with the two-stroke street bikes: comfort was more important than performance.

Part of this semi-touring marketing approach stemmed from necessity. The KH500 was slow; in fact, the factory had done a superb job of strangling the performance of the 500cc engine. It was now modernised with a new one-down and four-up gearshift pattern, but beneath its quiet, and very heavy, exhaust pipes it was a shadow of the violent, fuel-guzzling, 120mph monster of the '60s. Changes to the airbox and carbs sapped some brake horsepower from the three cylinder motor, and the new pipes did the rest. In truth, the preceding H1F probably never made the claimed 60bhp of the original H1, but the official KH500 figure of just 52bhp

KH500

The KH500 was a more touring-friendly triple, apart from its 30mpg fuel consumption.

THE KAWASAKI TRIPLES BIBLE

Mike Gardner took his restored KH500 on a 2200 mile tour in 2009: no problems apart from a broken clutch cable. (Courtesy Zeephoto.com)

at 7000rpm (down 1000rpm from the H series) didn't set pulses racing with triples fans. The unlucky West Germans even got a restricted 50bhp edition to meet their insurance brackets.

Rider magazine took the KH500 on a road trip to 'Frisco and found it managed 29mpg, drank a US pint of two-stroke oil every 500 miles, and could only hit a sluggish 95mph flat out, although, admittedly, the bike had a touring windscreen fitted to it. Meanwhile, in the UK, *Which Bike?* recorded the KH500 as capable of 112mph, which was fast for a 500cc class bike, but a good 10mph down on the original '68 H1's claimed 124mph.

The new KH500 made its way to the US market first in late '75. Testers and public

KH500

alike were no doubt pleased the bike now featured a conventional gear shift pattern, but there were teething troubles with the new layout.

Kawasaki issued a service bulletin to US dealers as soon as the KH500 was launched in December '75, as there was a potential problem with finding neutral in the revised gearbox. The bulletin sent to dealers read as follows:

"The 1976 KH500 has a neutral positioning bolt on the upper crankcase. On some early KH500s, the positioning bolt boss (In the crankcase body) was machined too short. Installation of the positioning bolt and pin in a short boss may interfere with normal gear changing. (A diagram shows a transmission measured in neutral. From the top indent in the shift drum detent plate to the top of the boss should be 22mm, 20mm is bad.)

"The factory action is to install an extra gasket and washer under the positioning bolt. Dealer action is to reinstall added parts when servicing units, and check for added parts any time the neutral positioner is removed or a customer complains of shifting problems on an affected unit."

Otherwise, the KH500 A8 proved durable, although it's fair to say it attracted a less crazy type of rider than its H1 series predecessors. The factory issued an upgraded exhaust stud in '78 for all triples, by the way, made of chrome-moly steel. Owners had found that the later triples with rubber-mounted engines could apply extra force to the studs, thus causing breakage. In fact, three studs broke on the test ride bike featured in *Rider* magazine.

The KH500 had a rubber-mounted engine, but testers still noted vibration coming through the re-shaped footpegs and handlebar grips. There was confusion over the bike's weight, with figures of 423lb and 428lb dry, plus a hefty 452lb wet, listed in various magazines. It was supposedly a lighter machine than the H1F, which had a dry weight of 438lb, but with the extra gusseting on the KH500's frame and essentially much the same

Brochure showing the '76 line-up.

This British KH500 has a split seat, a typical problem on many '70s Japanese machines. The fork gaiters were a common accessory from the era. (Courtesy Steve Brown)

A restored KH500 from Holland.

45

The Kawasaki Triples Bible

engine and chassis equipment, it's hard to see how Kawasaki saved 10lb, even with losing the hydraulic steering damper.

The new seat was slightly lower than on the H1F model, but generally considered less comfortable, due to its rounded profile. Pillions will definitely slide forward under braking because of the slope at the back of the saddle. The front disc was a new design on the KH500, taken from the Z1 and with new pads, another step along the road of making brakes work in the wet and not squeal in the dry. There was a lug on the right-hand fork leg for an optional second disc brake.

Although the KH500 was now seen as something of an all-rounder, it still retailed in the USA with just one mirror; the second mounting hole was blanked off. It sold for just under $1500 in the USA and £749 in the UK, below the £885 of a Honda CB550F, or £802.56 of a Suzuki GT550 triple. The KH500 was a reasonable seller in its day across Europe and the USA, mainly due to retail price and the reputation of its ass-kicking H1 predecessor.

But, at the end of '76, the party was over for the original Kawasaki triple; the 500 was dropped and only the KH250/400 series bikes remained in production.

1976 KH500 A8 spotter's guide

The bike can have either NGK B9HS or B9HCS, competition plugs, both are correct as the factory changed the OE plug early in the model year.

Three stripe graphics on tank and tail piece, colours were Copper and Deep Burgundy.

19 inch front wheel retained.

Different seat for '76, thin strip detail on the side.

Side reflectors and high handlebars for US-spec bikes.

Distinctive large oval shaped rear light lens.

Lug on right hand fork leg for optional extra disc brake.

Engine numbers: KAE117100 on.
Frame numbers: H1F47000 on.

1976 KH500 A8 collector's notes

Some KH500 A8 models will have been registered in December '75 in the USA and throughout '77, as dealers gradually sold off any remaining stock once production ceased. More of the Copper, or brown-coloured KH500s seem to have been sold in North America; the Burgundy red appears more common in Europe. Like other triples, the KH500 numbers in Europe have been boosted by imports from the USA during the '90s.

Total production can be estimated in the 9000-10,000 unit range for the KH500 model, one of Kawasaki's top-selling models within the triples range. It is hard to imagine the factory gearing up for full-scale production of much less than 10,000 units. This was a significantly updated machine and there was no H2 750 to steal sales from it, either.

The spirit of the triples

Sometimes, history isn't about sprockets, piston clearances, or who finished where in some sepia-toned race results. It's the experiences of owners, everyday riders hooked on the raw speed, dance-with-the-devil handling, and charismatic, clattering soundtrack of the triples. These motorcycles get under the skin.

A restored KH500 from Germany in Deep Burgundy.

KH500

Mike Gardner from Florida sums it up pretty well: "I'm 54 years old now and I've always loved the two-stroke triples. I live in Florida and have worked at the Space Centre for the past thirty years. In October 2009 I took my KH500 to Virginia to see my brother – some 2200 miles. The bike did great, except for a clutch cable breaking. I made it to a Honda dealer in North Carolina and we used a dirt bike cable that worked.

"The trip took longer than I thought, because so many people wanted to talk about the bike. Everyone had some kind of story about their dad or uncle, maybe a friend who was hurt or got in trouble with the cops on a triple. Every time I rode it, I'd get a 'thumbs-up' on the road.

"I got my first triple in 1974, it was a 1973 H1 and I paid $1000.00 for it. Nice bike, but it didn't handle too well. There were a lot of triples running around then: you either loved them or hated them. The Harley boys would give me a hard time about the ring-ding sound. I'd just leave them in a cloud of smoke.

"I bought my KH500 in October '97 for $250.00. I completely tore it down and did full restoration on it. It took 200 hours. It came out pretty nice, only have 1700 dollars in it. I ride it a couple times a week. I sometimes look back at photos of me in the summer of 1974, and check out the hair, clothes and helmet. Crazy days."

Mike Gardner in '74 on his H1E 500, which inspired him to pick up a KH500 and restore a Kawasaki triple three decades later.

Visit Veloce on the web – www.veloce.co.uk / www.velocebooks.com
Details of all books in print • Special offers • New book news • Gift vouchers • Forum

47

CHAPTER FOUR

THE H2 SERIES

The launch ads for the H2 were all about speed.

The H2, or Mach IV as it was known in the North American market, was one of the first true Superbikes of the '70s. Sure, Honda had got things started with the CB750 in '69, but the Mach IV 'melted minds' when it appeared in late '71 across the USA, with its claimed 74bhp and 125mph performance. It was also a difficult machine to handle, and became known as the 'Widow-maker' in the States, and 'Bara Volante' (flying coffin) in Italy.

More than any other machine, except perhaps the original H1 500, the 750 triple cemented the Kawasaki reputation for scarily fast, good-looking, no-holds-barred motorcycles. A machine that inspired a new generation of wheelie-popping, brash young riders, the H2 definitely helped Kawasaki sell thousands of KH250s off the back of its big brother's howling charisma. Finally, the H2 was another nail in the coffin for the British bike industry, as it made the Trident and Commando look like the '60s throwbacks they undoubtedly were.

Back in '71, the open road seemed to belong to the high performance two-stroke.

48

THE H2 SERIES

1971-72 H2

Get it on

Whilst Marc Bolan and T Rex were at the top of the charts in the summer of '71 with *Get It On* (known as *Bang a Gong* in the USA), Kawasaki was putting the finishing touches to its new range of triples. The Mach II 350 was going to be launched first in the USA, followed closely by the Mach IV 750.

Originally, Kawasaki had considered making a 650 triple, as thinking in the late '60s was that an air-cooled two-stroke above 500cc was too prone to seizure to be a viable production bike. Once Honda had established the 750cc class as the premier division for sporting motorcycles, however, that idea went out the window: Kawasaki had to make a 750 triple to trounce the four-strokes made by Norton, Triumph, and Honda.

The machine it built was closely based on the Mach III, but had a gutsier, less revvy engine inside a strengthened frame. The Mach IV made a claimed 74bhp at 6800rpm (later, Kawasaki literature revised this figure to a modest 71bhp), developed much lower than the 8000rpm peak of the Mach III. This was a good way of making the bike run a bit cooler, and therefore less likely to seize.

The motor had alloy cylinders and heads with cast iron liners, plus pistons and rings with a high silicon content to withstand the heat. How hot? The University of Osaka ran a series of two-stroke tests in the early '70s, and discovered that the temperature just above an exhaust port was 470 degrees Fahrenheit. This is why air-cooled two-strokes are prone to seizing – one race team engineer described H2R engines as "time bombs; it was a matter of luck if they held together or went nuclear on you."

Inside the Mach IV engine the crankshaft had the same 120 degree throw, but the round flywheels were replaced with 'pork chop'-shaped sections on the Mach IV. It's an arguably more efficient crank assembly design than simple 360 degree flywheels, and necessary in a big, two-stroke motor. Less weight, less inertia is always good. Compression was fairly low, too, with a modest 7:1 ratio. The new 750 breathed in via three 30mm Mikuni carbs and the oil pump was metered by the throttle.

This and following page: The Tri-Stars campaign was one of the most memorable in motorcycle advertising during the '70s.

49

To beef up oil delivery to the engine, Kawasaki used a check valve to effectively split the two-stroke lubricant supply once the pump had delivered it to the bottom end. Crankcase pressure will send oil around an engine on its own, but Kawasaki's engineers were keen to assist delivery to specific areas with the 750 engine. Their ideas obviously worked, as the H2/Mach IV series engines are still running today in high numbers, despite the best efforts of many owners to destroy them.

As on the H1 500, primary drive was via straight-cut gears, which produce the typical Kawasaki soundtrack. The gearbox was tough (even when raced it usually withstood lots of abuse) but it had neutral at the bottom and a seven-plate clutch which wasn't really up to the job. The clutch on the road-based Mach IV can regularly suffer slip, according to Rick Brett, who also notes that the H2 can sometimes jump out of first gear. One other RB tip is that the oil feed lines to the engine can leak, thus filling the bottom end with two-stroke lubricant.

The chassis was closely based on the H1, with a longer 55.5 inch wheelbase, extra bracing to the frame rails, and a 19 inch front, 18 inch rear rim. There was an attempt from the word go to provide more ground clearance on the H2 than early H1 models had, by setting the pipes closer to the motor and sweeping them up as soon as they cleared the footrest hangers. To a degree it worked, but the motor itself was still set too high and too far back for the bike's own good.

Cycle Guide tested the launch H2

bike in autumn '71 and pithily described the high speed handling as "like there was a hinge in the middle." Meanwhile, *Supercycle* magazine crashed its bike after the back end stepped out on a corner and the resulting tank-slapper spat the rider off. As Kawasaki's brochures noted, the Mach IV was for experienced riders – and even they could get caught out sometimes by the big 750.

All the US magazines drag raced the Mach IV, of course, and times in the 12.3 to 12.8 range were recorded. Kawasaki put a pro drag racer on board and advertised a 12 second dead quarter mile, which was possible on the relatively low gearing the Mach IV ran. *Bike* magazine in the UK recorded a 12.5 time; *Motorcycle Sport* didn't bother with such fripperies, but did note that the H2 had "quite singular acceleration," although it refused to go faster than 112mph.

The bike's torque impressed testers, and is one of the best reasons for buying an H2 today. It is perhaps the easiest of all the triples to ride relatively gently. Like the Suzuki GT750 of the same era, the H2/Mach IV makes peak torque at 5500rpm, quite low in the rev range. Incidentally, this is exactly the same point at which the 1950s DKW/Elva 750cc two-stroke car engine reached peak power. As testers noted at the time, the peak torque figure on the Kawasaki 750 was lower than on a Norton Commando, and made the H2 an easy bike to ride if you backed off the throttle slightly. Details like the wide seat, decent sized front disc brake, and better than average headlamp also made life more bearable, almost safe, for the rider. Best of all, the H2 was cheap, at just $1386 in the USA and £700 in the UK, substantially less than the superbike benchmark machine, Honda's CB750.

Of course, very few people could buy an H2 in Europe in '72, as supplies were fairly limited. Some 113 bikes made it to the UK, according to data from Agrati Sales, whilst Sidemm in France probably took three times that number, and Henk Vink in Holland and Marino Abba in Italy about the same. But these were tiny sales figures

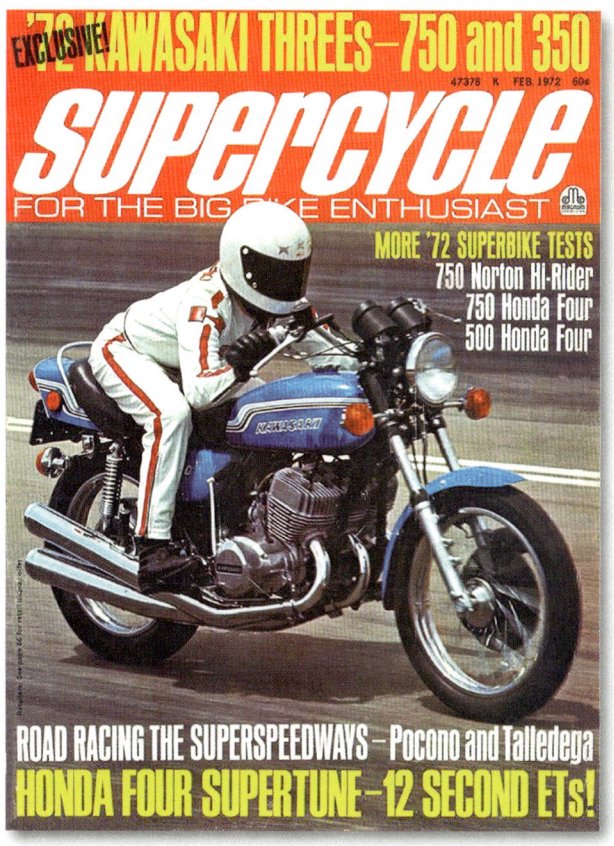

THE KAWASAKI TRIPLES BIBLE

Most of the US H2 models from '71 and '72 were in Candy Blue, although Candy Gold 750SS machines were selling in Japan and Europe.

compared to the thousands sold in the USA and Canada. North America was where Kawasaki had to make a big impression – there was no way it was going to starve America of 750s, when it was planning a massive assault on the racetrack there in '72 with the H2R.

The budget for the 'Year of the Tri-Stars' marketing campaign was probably about 100 times what Kawasaki spent in total in Europe that year. Kawasaki Japan upped its overall bike production from 150,000 units in '70 to 209,000 for '71, the first year that the 'Big Four' manufacturers exported over half a million motorcycles above 250cc between them. The majority of Kawasaki production went to the USA.

The Mach IV was also launched as the 750SS in Japan, and marketed as a kind of pleasant 'let's visit a museum' type of touring machine. The image was a far cry from the disco-booted chicks used to sell the 500SS a few years previously. The mood in Japan had changed. In 1970, the Japanese government passed a batch of licence and safety laws which would reduce the consumer base for big bikes within the decade by making it increasingly hard to get a big bike licence at all. Schools were also being instructed to teach their pupils not to ride motorcycles, or accept a lift on one – ever. The 750SS sold in small numbers, as Japan was essentially a small capacity mass motorbike market then. The 750 class was very much 'for expert riders.'

It may have been described as a 'tourer' in some of the marketing blurb, but people road raced the H2. Burgess and Steele won the Castrol 6 Hour endurance in '72 on a production class H2, Collinson and Galbraith hammered it to victory until '75 in New Zealand street circuit events, and many brave individuals 'gave it a go' in production class events worldwide.

Dave Chisma raced his H2 in Canada. "I was a mechanic at a Kawasaki dealer in Kamloops, British Columbia, so it was good for me to race the H2. It was very quick. The only thing that stopped me winning races was a lack of talent. In 1973 I was often a front-runner for at least part of the race, but as a 19-year old in my first full season I had a few DNFs, typically caused by not listening closely enough to the complaints of my pipes scraping the tarmac. In 1974 I upgraded to a new model, but it was never as quick as the original. And then the Kawasaki shop burned down and took the bike with it."

Under production racing rules then, there wasn't much scope for tuning, but Dave recalls some tweaks he made to his H2. "I couldn't change the port dimensions, but I did polish the ports and ensure the path from crankcase to port was smooth and even in its cross-section. The rules prohibited modifying the intake system, but the H2 always seemed to go better with the rubber intake silencer removed. This was a common cheat back then. Plus, I removed the glass-mat packing from the exhaust."

Dave also had a spectacular method of cleaning gunk from the H2's pipes. "Prior to a race I would always pull the pipes off and clean them out, which would involve heating the interior with an oxy-acetylene flame until the carbon inside the pipe glowed. Then I'd direct a stream of air inside the pipe and it would become a huge blowtorch until all the junk was burnt off – this was best done out of doors!"

THE H2 SERIES

The H2 became known as the 'widow-maker' and its handling was supposedly dire, but is this myth or reality? Dave reckons it was a capable production race machine for the times. "Chassis setup was standard, with only changes to spring preload and fork oil. I was told that any bike's handling was only bad if it made you crash or slow down. I reckoned the H2's handling was more frightening for spectators than it was for me. It would often wiggle a bit, but never uncontrollably. I could lean it over until everything dragged – and then crash. One of the chassis tweaks that I felt was helpful was to shim the engine mounts so that you could secure the engine in place without distorting the frame. I think there was a Kawasaki Tech Bulletin about this mod later."

Teething troubles

There was a reasonably rapid reaction to some of the initial troubles the H2/Mach IV suffered. Kawasaki fitted new brake pads and a shim to try and cure brake squeal, applied to the H2 from chassis number H2F10491 on, with US dealers instructed to retro fit the fix at service time on '71-72 model Mach IVs.

In spring '72, Kawasaki issued a new set of shims for the engine mountings, after noting those on early models could work loose due to vibration. All models up to engine number H2E09082 were affected, so a retro fit kit was offered via the dealer network. A supplementary rectifier was specified from May '72, as some had discharged the battery on models up to engine number H2E13265. A larger pinion nut was fitted in June '72 to deal with a clutch knocking noise caused by excess play. The new nut is 29mm, the old 27mm; engine number H2E05228 on had the new pinion nut fitted at the factory.

The factory redesigned the rear

Dave Chisma racing his H2 in Canada in the early '70s.

Cycle magazine rated the Mach IV "King of the quarter mile."

53

brake mechanism to cure sponginess, or lack of feel. The brake lever and the torque link were changed after frame number H2F05215. The latter parts can be retro fitted to early Mach IVs.

One of the more interesting changes was the switch from Yokohama to Dunlop front tyres in autumn 1972 for the US-spec Mach IV machines. Europeans made do with Yokohamas, but, due to complaints about speed wobbles when drag racing, a Dunlop 19 inch, 3.25 section F6 tyre was specified as OE fitment. Kawasaki instructed dealers to check that front axles were tight, as some 'speed wobbles' were traced to incorrect torque settings – the correct setting is 55 ft/lb; 26psi in the front and 31psi rear were the recommended factory tyre pressures, too.

Candy Gold H2 was imported to Italy by Genoa-based Marino Abbo.

In late '72, the Mach IV and Mach III received a new O-ring kit for the oil pump to stop the right-hand cylinder smoking excessively after an oil pump leakage. The problem could be serious, with oil being forced back into the pump in some cases, and causing seizure.

Frustratingly, Kawasaki neglected to say from which engine number the new improved O-ring kit was fitted during '72. According to Kawasaki's tech bulletins, the only way to spot the modification is that the pump chamber was fractionally reduced to 13.7mm diameter from the original 14.1mm, to allow the O-ring to bed in that bit tighter.

There may have been a problem with the throttle assembly on early H2 models, as well. Dave Chisma recalls a tragic incident at a Canadian racetrack. "The early H2 had what I regarded as a fatal flaw. One of the first times I saw one race in the production class was in 1972 at Westwood Motorsport Park, when a rider died in an accident. At the time I thought it was really strange: I saw him at high speed on the straight heading towards a hairpin bend. Instead of braking hard the rider just sat up and went off the bend; he died in the forest.

"I don't know if it's connected, but I believe the early production H2s had a throttle assembly that could rotate if it wasn't securely fastened to the handlebars, so, if you cranked the throttle hard enough you could move it around. The problem then was the throttle lock screw would align with the front brake lever and so prevent the brake from being applied fully. In later shipments, there was a locking pin that fitted into a hole in the handlebars to keep the throttle assembly in place."

By modern standards, the H2 suffered few faults, but they were caused by exactly the same problem as with modern automotive manufacturing; too much out-sourcing to a myriad of supplier companies, plus a frantic rush into production with new models. Kawasaki was already a vast industrial empire in the early '70s, arguably much more so than any of its rivals. Relatively little budget and time was devoted to the motorcycle division, and much of the technical development of component parts was farmed out. For example, the early H1 500's CDI problems were essentially a supplier quality control issue which wasn't spotted before the bike's launch, and dealt with rapidly enough. Too much trust was placed in suppliers getting the job right first time, every time.

As we will see in the chapter on the H2R race bikes, this faith was misplaced and probably cost Kawasaki some important race wins.

THE H2 SERIES

1971-72 H2-Mach IV-750SS spotter's guide

US bikes had high 'bars and side reflectors; Japanese bikes, too.
Official colour was Pearl Candy Blue only for USA, some Candy Gold models for Japan, Europe, Africa and other markets.
Model should be fitted with a plunger-operated chain-oiler.
Twist-on type brake fluid reservoir.
Friction steering damper only, no hydraulic extra damper.
Kind of 'wee' bottle-shaped air scoop on top of airbox.
Engine numbers: H2E00001 on.
Frame numbers: H2F00001 on.

European store leaflet from '72: much the same copy was used in German, French, and Dutch brochures at the time.

1971-72 H-H2A collector's notes

Approximately 22,000 H2 machines were made, and the early '71 registered models will probably be the highest value machines in the long run. Anything which has truly original parts on it, rather than the many 'new old stock' replica pieces, is more collectable. That's not to say it's better to ride, of course, just more collectable because of its rarity.

The original paint may have faded, or changed hue slightly. Two examples of Candy Blue or Gold '72 models may look different, and this is normal; paint changes over time and it is possible there were variations in hue, as applied by the factory.

The H2 paintwork was designed by Molly (Rollin Sanders of California), who worked for custom car/bike builders and motorcycle racing motorcycle teams in the late '60s. Reportedly, Molly had to visit Kawasaki to help fine tune the process of applying the Candy and Pearl Candy coatings he devised, prior to the '71 model launches.

Although Kawasaki doesn't list it, some H2 models in '72 were definitely produced in Candy Gold and sold in most markets apart from the USA. Many examples exist in Europe to the present day and the Japanese 750SS brochure features a Candy Gold machine.

1973 H2A

The purple people-eater

After a successful launch of the H2, and the Z1 at the end of the year, Kawasaki really started '73 with some serious ambition. Its semi factory race operation, Team Hansen, became more or less a full factory effort, although many staff were essentially freelancers. It was expanded for the '73 season and featured riders like Yvon du Hamel, Gary Nixon, Cliff Carr, and Art Baumann. The Transatlantic Match races and Imola 200 were on the schedule, as well as the AMA series.

On the street the new A series triples made their debut early in the year, with their more sedate styling and relatively minor technical changes affecting the H2A.

The H2A was marketed across the USA as a big touring machine now, still fast with a claimed 12 second quarter mile time, but featuring a helmet lock, locking fuel cap, and a new, more integrated set of clocks complete with warning lights. Interestingly, Kawasaki actually put an speed vs fuel

55

THE KAWASAKI TRIPLES BIBLE

One of West Germany's biggest dealers, Detlev Louis of Hamburg, imported triples in the early '70s. According to German triples enthusiasts, Detlev was able to choose which models he wanted to import.

Restored H2A at the 2009 Classic Mechanics Show, with a handy steering damper attached.

Die kräftigste serienmäßige Supermachine in der 750 Klasse!

750 MACH IV model H2

THE H2 SERIES

consumption graph in its brochure which showed the H2A drinking the stuff at 20mpg. The company would come to regret that later in the year when all hell broke loose in the Middle East and the price of fuel shot up. Some road tests state that the exhausts had different internals to make the bike quieter, but this appears untrue: the pipes are the same as the first generation H2, according to UK Kawasaki triples club expert Malc Anderson.

Cycle magazine tested the new H2A in early '73 and found that the bike made a healthy 64.5bhp at the back wheel on the dyno. This was the highest power figure out of a seven-strong superbike group, and the triple made more grunt than the Z1. Hard to believe? Definitely, but *Cycle* had all the engines stripped and checked after the test – the H2A was bone stock, reportedly. The H2A was also the cheapest of the big motorcycles on test, at just $1400; the Z1 was a cool $2000.

The H2A wasn't perfect, of course. The bike had the O-ring problem in its oil pump, supposedly fixed at the start of its production run, but there was an ongoing issue with loosening of the backing plate for the oil pump. The pump could leak oil, causing excessive smoking, or starvation to one cylinder and then piston seizure. New banjo bolts were fitted to the pump's backing plate from engine number H2E30126 on, says Kawasaki.

The forks can emit a clunking noise on H2A models, and new fork damper cylinders were fitted from 1974 to remedy this. The H2A series had new fork seals from the start of its run as well, as they were liable to pop after a few wheelies. Chassis number H2F19037 was the official changeover date for the seals, by the way.

The H2 series was given new carb settings from November 1972, with the main jet going from 105R to 97.5R, and dealers instructed to set the air screw at one and a half turns out, rather than one and a quarter, whilst the starter jet increased from 40 to 70. Pilot and air jets stayed the same. Modified carbs should have H2-2 marked on them to identify the different settings used.

According to Kawasaki, a set of shims was added to the H2A series gearbox to try and prevent the bike jumping out of gear occasionally. All five gears had potential problems and Kawasaki USA dealerships were given precise instructions on how to re-shim the gears to make engagement more positive.

Later in '73, Kawasaki issued new instructions on curing problems with the CDI stator unit. A typical fault was shorting out, mainly due to water getting in. A new gasket and cover sealant was recommended alongside a list of checks and wiring diagrams for dealer mechanics to follow. Incidentally, the '73 H1D stator assembly can be fitted to the H2 and H2A.

The H2A wasn't as big a seller in Europe as in the USA, and a reasonable guess at numbers would be under 2000 units for western Europe. A few hundred examples may have made it to markets such as South Africa. The UK took just 30 examples, officially.

It was thoughtful of Kawasaki to alert customers to the vibration they may encounter at high speed.

1973 H2A spotter's guide
Official colours were Candy Gold and Candy Purple.
New clocks assembly and warning light console.
Metal trim on side of seat.
Lower handlebars for European models.
Chrome front mudguard, not painted.
Fuel tank may lack locking cap, factory seemed to use old parts on some H2A models.
Engine numbers: H2E23158 on.
Frame numbers: H2F23671 on.

THE KAWASAKI TRIPLES BIBLE

The H2A model from 1973.

Sidemm in France sold the H2 on the strength of its performance and reliability, proving it in several endurance races.

1974 H2B

Smoothing off the edges

For '74 Kawasaki gave the H2 a makeover that softened its character a little, although the bike still offered superb performance for its day. The engine received a few tweaks aimed at improving durability of the unit, and its exhaust emissions and noise were curtailed with new internals.

New oilways were drilled into the big ends, and different con-rods fitted. Kawasaki endured a string of con-rod failures in its H1R/H2R racing engines, so by '74 had sourced upgraded slotted rods, with a better hardening process undertaken by its supplier. Similar rods went into the H2B road model – a case of racing actually improving the production motorcycle. In its official H2B press literature, Kawasaki claimed that check valves were used on the H2B models to improve oil scavenging, but the H2 had check valves from the start of production. It's possible Kawasaki meant upgraded valves, similar to the ones fitted to the 500 series machines from 1974. It is equally possible it was simply wrong information from Kawasaki Japan.

The clutch was beefed up to try and minimise slip, and the gearbox retained the same shift pattern, with neutral at the bottom. The gears had been re-shimmed by the factory from '74 on to try and remedy the gear-jumping trait identified by early H2 owners. The H2B series also had a wider shift fork on third gear to make selection more positive.

One area of confusion concerns the

THE H2 SERIES

H2B's engine mountings. For example, in late '74, *Bike* magazine noted that there was a "definite tingle" above 5000rpm from the "rubber-mounted engine." But, according to Kawasaki, no H2 ever had a rubber-mounted motor.

That said, *Bike* got many test bikes from helpful dealer Davick Motique, and this particular H2B was one of them. Davick had changed the sparkplugs and the tyres on the demo H2B bike to improve matters; maybe it fitted H1 rubber mounts, as the H1E for '74 gained that useful addition?

The B model also had the old friction steering damper replaced by an hydraulic type, and the steering was altered slightly by kicking out the forks an inch (the aim was to make the bike more stable, and less wheelie-prone). The H2B was being sold as a kind of touring bike, but with rocketship speed.

Visually, the bike changed quite a bit. The tailpiece was a different shape and a bit smaller, whilst the fuel tank and side panels changed, too. The oil tank filler cap was now hidden from vandals' fingertips by being located beneath the seat, instead of on top of the side panel. Again, US and Canadian bikes had raised handlebars, whilst most European models had lower 'bars. Although not officially listed by Kawasaki, it made the bike in two-tone brown for the US market.

Some UK, French and Italian H2Bs could be bought with the higher US-style 'bars, by the way – there was no real consistency in Kawasaki's machine specification in the mid '70s. A second disc brake remained an optional extra, and some UK-spec bikes might have had a front number plate, as well as a rear plate fitted from new.

UK numbers on the H2B are officially 100 units. It's possible some direct imports came in as Agrati had ceased importing in late '73, and the fledgling Kawasaki UK operation was then running from a hotel suite in London. KMUK became operational in summer 1974, so anyone who really wanted a Kawasaki earlier in the year had to approach a dealer with contacts abroad.

Numbers across Europe for the H2B can be estimated at around 1700 units as '74 was a tough year in which to sell a 20mpg motorcycle. Many countries – even the USA – had to ration petrol early in '74 as gas stations ran dry. Petrol prices went up by 50 per cent within weeks. The UK declared a state of emergency over the winter of '73-74, and issued fuel ration books to road users. Given this chaos, it's remarkable that Kawasaki sold the best part of 10,000 H2B models worldwide. Maybe they were snapped up by oil barons ...

Heavily modified H2B from the USA in the rare and sometimes unloved Candy Brown colour.

1974 H2B spotter's guide
Official colours were Candy Gold and Candy Lime. Candy Brown for US only.
Still has plunger chain lube pump behind side panel.
New tank, seat and tail section.
Oil tank filler now under the seat.
New switchgear, choke moves to the left 'bar.
Hydraulic steering damper replaces friction type.
Engine number: H2E32401.
Frame number: H2F32201.

1975 H2C

From wild one to easy rider
The last of the H2 line was perhaps the

59

The Kawasaki Triples Bible

easiest to ride, but lacked some of the fire and brimstone of the original H2.

The tech spec and road tests of the era make much of the longer wheelbase. In fact, the bike had exactly the same wheelbase as the preceding B model.

It's also worth noting that, as from the B series the H2 750's official power output was 71bhp, it seems just as 'restricted' as the C model that followed. There's also a question mark over when Kawasaki changed the way that two-stroke oil was metered into the H2 engine: late B model or start of the C models?

Officially, this new oil feed coincided with the introduction of the C model, but triples enthusiasts have found B models with the telltale oil lines to the carbs. The system was a kind of half pre-mix, half inject lube. Belt-and-braces in layman's terms, here's how it worked: as the throttle was opened, half the oil supply was fed into the float bowls of the carbs, and half went the usual route to the main bearings, where check valves and crankcase pressure did the work of sending the oil around the bottom end.

It's hard to see how this carb-fed oil could really have made the bike run with cleaner emissions, since surely the same

Restored H2C in the popular purple colour.

amount of oil (or more) was going into the motor, via the two feed methods? Perhaps the intention was simply to burn off some oil alongside the petrol in the combustion chamber, to reduce visible smoking, or help prevent seizures by pre-mixing the H2 motor? The exact reasoning behind the two-part oil feed system remains a mystery.

Cycle World found the H2C was only capable of a 13.06 quarter mile, with a 99.5mph terminal speed. Weight, now at 479lb wet, had crept up from the H2/H2A series. On the upside the magazine liked the Dunlop Gold Seal tyres, and was mildly impressed by the average 26mpg the H2C returned. Like the tester said, however, the H2 was "no longer King of the Superbikes."

Again, from the C model on, the steering damper is supposed to have been switched from the right- to the left-hand side. There are B and C models with the damper on either side; location appears to have depended on how the production line manager felt that day.

One minor problem worth mentioning is that centre stands can break on the H2 models, due, it seems, to a manufacturing weakness.

Despite its reduced performance the H2C model sold well, as almost everyone knew this would be the last big two-stroke from Kawasaki. The world had changed after the '73 oil crisis and there was no going back to the halcyon days of gas-guzzling, wheelie-popping, high speed motorcycles that encouraged all kinds of highway madness. The only choice open to anyone who wanted a slice of that superbike-sized, two-stroke glory was the '75 H2C.

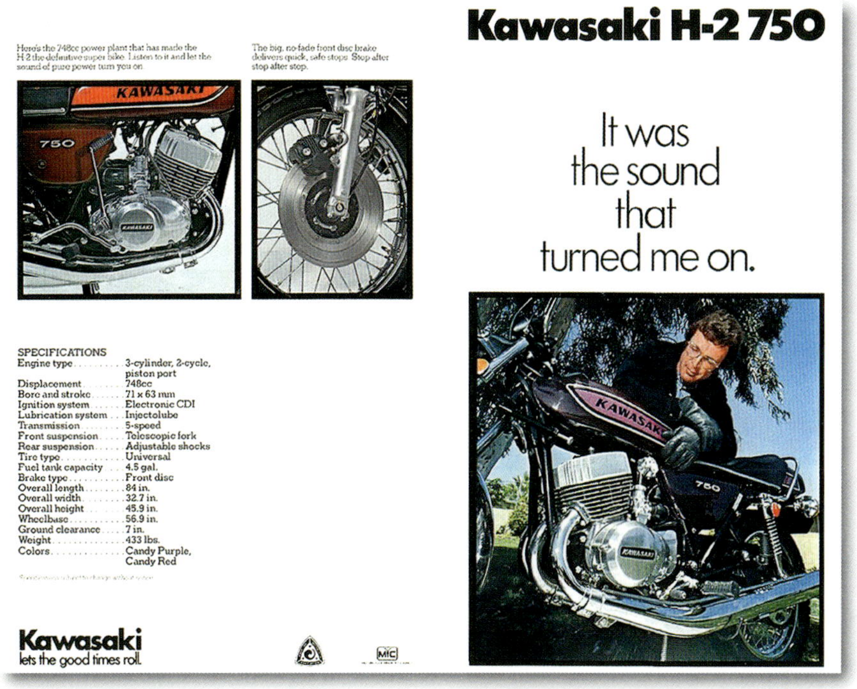

Kawasaki UK has lost the original sales figures for '75, but a reasonable guess would be about ten H2C models per dealer, and, as Kawasaki had appointed about 15 dealers by late '74, that makes around 150 units. The Z1 sold much better from late '74 on, having picked up the *MCN* Machine of The Year award at the end of '73: there was a much bigger profit margin on the Z1, too. Some H2Cs in the UK were registered as '76 new bikes; it took a while to run down stocks.

Above: By '75 the H2C was selling on its sound, despite the EPA forcing Kawasaki to make the bike quieter.

THE KAWASAKI TRIPLES BIBLE

Goodyear chose a Vetter-ised H2 to sell its tyres.

Part of Malc Anderson's triple collection and his favourite H2 to ride, the easygoing H2C.

THE H2 SERIES

Could Kawasaki have stuck with two-strokes if it had switched to water-cooling? Yes, for a few years. Although Kawasaki had built a running prototype, water-cooled, 750cc, two-stroke in '72, having closely studied Yamaha's GL750 at the '71 Tokyo Show, it – like all manufacturers – knew the days of the two-strokes per se were numbered. It was only a matter of time before the environmentalists and anti-noise lobby persuaded governments to kill them off. So, instead, Kawasaki water-cooled the H2R race machine for the '75 season, and made a small, liquid-cooled 250 which took the World Championship with Kork Ballington on board.

The H2C probably sold about 2500 units across Europe as motorcycling enjoyed a huge boom, encouraged by the excellent summers of '75 and '76. Countries like Cyprus, Greece, Spain and Portugal were beginning to import Kawasaki machines as well, as the corporate empire expanded on its Amsterdam bridgehead. Italian triples enthusiasts think that many of the 750s sold there between 1972 and 1975 found their way to Germany and Scandinavia in the '90s, incidentally.

The bulk of H2C production was sold to the USA, of course; at a guess, some 6000 units, with Canada probably taking about 10 per cent of the US total. Other markets that took significant quantities include Australasia, South Africa, and the Middle East.

1975 H2C spotter's guide
Official colours were Candy Purple and Super Candy Red.
Hydraulic steering damper can be seen on either side.
Some models registered in '76 as stocks sold off.
Engine numbers: H2E42827 on.
Frame numbers: H2F42547 on.

1974 H2B-1975 H2C collector's notes
Many of the later H2B/C models seem to have survived, perhaps due to the slightly older, less speed-crazed customer who bought them. The sheer cost of running the bike probably also meant that more affluent types owned the H2B/C.

Some parts are becoming extremely difficult to find now, and many owners have used the increasing range of NOS (new old stock) replica parts suppliers. As with British classic bikes, which have relied on hand-crafted, remanufactured spares for much of the last two decades, the same process of short run parts production will help keep Kawasaki triples on the road.

The prices for genuine, original H2 models, from A to C, are rising, and likely to rise still higher in the long term. It always was the most spectacular of the triples to look at, as well as the fastest production two stroke of the '70s. The later B and C models are easier to ride, and that makes it a classic you can actually enjoy. The earlier H2 is arguably the original 'widow-maker,' and perhaps the most collectable of all the triples – better than money in the bank; it's also a great deal more fun than a pension plan!

Triples fan Terje Aspmo shows how exciting a '70s bike is still.

This 750 triple was being raced at Bonneville Salt Flats in 2009 in the BUB Speed Trials. In the modified street class it reached speeds of 120-125mph. The rider reported no engine problems after four days of running.

CHAPTER FIVE

THE 350 S2 SERIES

The mid-sized Kawasaki two-strokes are both highly collectable, especially the 350 S2, and arguably the most civilised to ride of all the triples. The late model 400s, in both Emerald Green and Candy Lime Green, are perhaps amongst the best looking motorcycles of the '70s.

The medium class Kawasaki triples first appeared in summer '71, in the form of a typically hard accelerating, sexily-styled, yet slightly fragile machine.

350 S2

Small is beautiful

When the S2 was launched in 1971, the 350cc class was still hotly contested in GP road racing, and many European riders saw a 350 as a stepping-stone between the learner 250s and the bigger 500-650 twins.

The Japanese had a slightly different take on the 350 class, and wanted to make mid-sized motorbikes that stood on their own merit, rather than a stopgap measure. Machines like the Yamaha RD350, Bridgestone 350, and Suzuki GT380 all demonstrated how rapidly the Japanese were learning to manufacture high performance bikes that could seriously challenge the arthritic big British and Harley twins of the early '70s.

Kawasaki was going full throttle in '71. On track, the big 750 H2R was starting to scream its way to the insane side of 170mph, battling against the Suzuki, BSA,

The Japanese brochure shot for the new 350SS and 250SS models of 1972.

THE KAWASAKI TRIPLES BIBLE

Above, left: Cycle Guide tested the 350 S2 and loved it.

Above, right: UK importer Agrati was keen to let everyone know it had stocks of the new S2, but forgot to mention that these were probably in single figures.

and Triumph triples in the fledgling F750 category, and on the speed bowl circuits of the USA. The road range of triples, from 250cc to 750cc, reached fruition and were ready to launch as '71 progressed. Kawasaki's reputation for outrageous performance, unique noise and 'real men only need apply' handling was about to be cemented in every rider's mind.

The 350 S2 was visually part of this new 'family' of three cylinder motorcycles, sharing the same styling as the first S1, H2 and '72 H1 models. In North American markets the S2 was known as the Mach II, and in Japan it was designated the 350-SS.

The two available colours were Pearl Candy Red and Pearl White. The US was the main target market for Kawasaki, just as it had been for the original H1 500, and the advertising budget for the S2 was large. Kawasaki lowered the gear ratios on US-spec S2 models to make sure they impressed journalists and public alike with rapid acceleration. It also ran for 24 hours at Ontario Raceway to prove its reliability. In the US market, a 350 was usually seen as a novice class machine, so the bike had an uphill struggle to win over 'sporty' riders. Initial sales were a struggle on the S2 across the USA, especially when the H2 750 was launched. which totally blew everyone away.

It was a similar story across Europe, where relatively few 350 S2 models were sold in '71 and '72. The UK and Republic of Ireland importer, Agrati Sales, officially listed 111 units of the S2 and 165 examples sold the following year. Agrati was told that its UK importer contract was being terminated in '73, so there are no reliable figures available on the S2A numbers. UK Kawasaki triples expert Rick Brett thinks it might have been "around ten, a dozen maybe."

Accurate numbers for UK registered

The 350 S2 series

Kawasaki bikes are difficult to assess pre-1974 (when KMUK was formed) for two reasons. Firstly, Agrati was not that methodical in its administration, and, secondly, some extra 'unofficial' triples were dealer imported. From the mid '60s until KMUK's launch in late '74, various UK dealers and a few production road racers were approaching C Itoh & Co in London (Kawasaki Heavy Industry's iron ore shipping agent), and even Kawasaki Japan directly, and buying batches of bikes.

These numbers were low volume, ranging from a handful to as many as 60-odd in any one year, but it's highly likely that this practice continued in the UK market, even after Agrati Sales was appointed UK importer in 1971.

Technically a bit of a twin

The new S2 350 was launched alongside the H2 and 500 H1B in the USA in late summer '71, with 'The Year of the Tri-Stars' advertising campaign aimed at new bike buyers of '72. The 350 made its way to Europe a few months later, joined by its near identical twin, the S1 250. The two smaller triple cylinder bikes were essentially the same model – the S2 is just one pound heavier than the S1 and, apart from engine internals, there are very few differences.

The S2 had a 346.2cc engine, with a 53x52.3mm bore and stroke, running 7.3:1 compression ratio. The engine featured a built-up crankshaft assembly, with caged roller bearings, substantial crankshaft balance weights, and steel pistons and liners. The five speed gearbox was a new one-down, four-up shift pattern, rather than having neutral at the bottom of the five speeds, as on the first H1 500 triples. Claimed peak power was 45bhp at 8000rpm.

The S1/S2 gearbox is tough, running needle and roller bearings throughout, but it does have a weak area; the selector forks. These can wear easily, causing the bike to jump out of gear under hard acceleration. The motor also has an annoying sludge trap in its gearbox which can attract any nasty metal debris, holding it there until an inevitable build-up causes serious problems. The entire bottom end of the engine – crankshaft assembly, gearbox, clutch, etc – is identical to the S1 250.

A four pint (imperial) oil tank feeds the injection lube system on the S2, with a gear-driven oil pump linked to the throttle forcing lubricant into the motor via the intake ports. There was also a feed from the pump to the left-hand main bearings, with oil then

The 350 S2 had a real marketing push in the USA, in stark contrast to its launch across Europe.

67

THE KAWASAKI TRIPLES BIBLE

moving across to the right-hand bearings before crankcase pressure forced it upward. This differed from the H1 500, where all the two-stroke oil was delivered to the bottom end, with crankcase pressure and transfer ports doing the distribution.

The lubrication system on the S2 works okay, but, like all two-strokes of the era, it was a fragile motor and demanded top quality oil – rare in 1971. Plenty of 350s burned up sparkplugs, seized, holed pistons, etc, especially if ridden hard or raced.

According to Kevin Cameron, former Kawasaki race technician, the smaller triples were built to a tight budget from the start. "For a street bike, making short trips around town, the S1/S2 is fine. But those who tried racing them in the '70s soon discovered that they seized, or suffered ignition problems. If the 250/350 had come in an R version, with chrome cylinder liners, close ratio 'box, upgraded CDI ignition, slotted con-rods, and silver-plated, caged roller bearings at the crank, then they could have challenged the Yamahas. But when tuned, the stock S2 was simply a less reliable motorcycle – and barely any faster."

A little detail which betrays

This page and opposite: The lavish 'Year of the Tri-Stars' brochure in the USA for the 350 Mach II, launched in late '71 across the US dealer network, although technically a '72 model.

THE 350 S2 SERIES

FIRST IN SPACE WITH A 350 THREE
45 horsepower gives enough thrust for a SS 1/4 mile time of just 13.6 seconds. 112 mph top speed means plenty of reserve for normal driving situations. 30.74 ft-lb of torque

BUILT TO TRAVEL THE GALAXIES
Low curb weight of 329 pounds. Quick, light handling. Double-triangulated twin-cradle tube frame keeps the power trained on the ground. Accurate, close-ratio five speed transmission gives a gear for any speed or traffic condition.

LIGHT-YEARS AHEAD STYLING
Looks that match the TriStar power. Three GP mosport chamber-type mufflers upswept at the rear for increased ground clearance in turns. Finished with two-tone sonic striping to set the mood for this new superstar. And the spoiler section with enclosed taillight continues the styling motif to the rear of the machine – all the competition will ever see. Tilted glare-shielded instruments designed for instant visibility tell the rider his speed/tach relationship at a glance. Double seat with passenger G rail. Slim-leg chromed forks. All set off in Pearl Candy Red. Looks that say "Blast off for the stars!"

NEWEST TRISTAR DESIGN
The MACH III has been the most successful 500 ever built – now an all-new 350 Three joins it in the TriStar fleet. Top middleweight action in the MACH II, with jet-smooth response from its engine. Better combustion and cooling from the tri-cylinder design. A fantastic power-to-weight ratio of 45 hp/329 lbs. The weight factor of just 329 pounds means performance unlike any other 350 – and better than other machines twice its size. JATO-like acceleration, modular styling, comfortable riding positions – the MACH II is the brightest new star in its class.

missiles the MACH II up the steepest mountain road, winding like a turbine, without tiring. The superb crank balance of the three-cylinder layout keeps vibration to a minimum.

Kawasaki SPECIFICATIONS

PERFORMANCE
Max. speed	112 mph
Acceleration	SS 1/4 mile: 13.6 sec
Climbing ability	40°
Braking distance	39 ft/31 mph
Min. turning radius	82.6 in.

ENGINE
Type	2-cycle, 3-cylinder, piston valve
Displacement	346.2 cc (21.19 cu. in.)
Bore and stroke	2.09 x 2.06 in.
Compression ratio	7.3:1
Max. horsepower	45 hp/8,000 rpm
Max. torque	30.74 ft-lb/7,000 rpm
Ignition system	Battery and coil
Starting system	Kick
Lubrication	SUPERLUBE (automatic oil injection)

TRANSMISSION
Type	5-speed, constant mesh, return shift
Clutch	Wet, multi-disc

DIMENSIONS
Length, overall	79.0 in.
Width, overall	31.5 in.
Height, overall	43.0 in.
Wheelbase	52.5 in.
Ground clearance	6.5 in.
Weight	329 lbs
Fuel tank capacity	3.7 U.S. gal
Oil tank capacity	1.6 U.S. qt

FRAME
Type	Tubular, double cradle
Suspension: Front	Telescopic fork
Rear	Swing arm
Tire size: Front	3.00-18 4PR
Rear	3.50-18 4PR

Specifications subject to change without notice.

Printed in Japan

some cost-cutting by Kawasaki on the 250/350 engine design is the lack of bridges on the cylinder head fins. These were fitted to the H1 500 in '68 to reduce noise and vibration. On the S3 400, rubber rings were fitted between the head fins to try and reduce the high rpm vibes, and noise, common to S2 models. It might sound a trivial issue, but as the S2 models develop nearly all their useful power between 6000 and 8000rpm, decent progress required lots of revs. Apart from the vibration wearing down the rider, it also caused parts to work loose on the bikes occasionally.

The use of three coils and three sets of points was another budget-conscious measure, which makes the S2 susceptible to erratic running. Everything must be spot-on for pin-sharp throttle response, and the metal plug caps were prone to shorting out in heavy rain. Incidentally, sparkplugs fitted back in '71 were NGK B9HS grade, with a spare set provided beneath the seat. The S2 needed the spares as typical hard riding could necessitate plug replacement every 500-1000 miles.

By the way, the '71 and '72 S2 models had a toolkit located in the tailpiece. There was a large gap under the seat which allowed this tool kit to slide across the rear mudguard and drop onto the road – hence original, and complete, tool kits are rare items for the S2/S1 series.

The wet, five-plate clutch came in for criticism in some road tests at the time of the 350 S2's launch, but some of that was undoubtedly due to repeated drag starts to set quarter mile times, particularly in US motorcycle magazines. That said, the later 400 S3 features a six-plate clutch. The clutch can rattle around at tickover, but is simply part of the triple's usual engine noise levels.

The S2 350 breathed in via three Mikuni VM24mm carbs, with a paper element air filter located in the airbox, set under the seat. There are three plastic intake tubes linking the airbox to the carbs, and their propensity to perish – and ham-fisted owner maintenance – mean that they crack, or warp, causing air leaks.

Both the 250 and 350 S-series triples can suffer repeated carb synchronisation problems, more noticeable on the smaller, less powerful engines than the 500 or 750 triples. Like most two-strokes of the era, the S2 requires constant checking and re-setting to keep it in peak tune; carbs, plugs, plug caps, points, air filter – the lot. The early S2 machines suffered from rattly clutches, and a factory shim kit was sent out from December '71 to try and resolve the problem.

The Kawasaki Triples Bible

This restored 350 S2 is another show winner from UK enthusiast Malc Anderson.

After the electronic ignition set-up fitted on the 500cc H1 back in '68, road testers of the '71 were surprised that the 350 S2 had three coils and sets of points. True, the 500 H1 had to have points in the UK market because the Post Office insisted on them, but it did seem a bit of a backward step. Kawasaki claimed a power output of 45bhp at 8000rpm for the S2, with a theoretical top speed of 112mph.

It made for great advertising copy, but the S2's top speed was a little exaggerated. *Cycle* magazine in the USA recorded 95mph, whilst *Cycle Guide* noted that the launch 350 S2 model could manage a true 92mph, with the speedo needle flickering above 100mph. *Motorcyclist Illustrated* in the UK noted, however, that it was impossible to rev the S2 above 9000rpm in top, but this still gave a more than respectable 107mph. It's possible that the European S2 models were geared differently, as the US market was obsessed with quarter mile times, so a European S2 may well have been some 10-15mph faster.

Embarrassingly for Kawasaki, the new Mach II was a slower accelerating bike than the outgoing A7 Avenger, in spite of lower gearing. *Cycle* magazine posted a 14.3 second quarter for the old Avenger, whilst a modest 14.8 was the best time for the new triple. The difficulty was getting the S2 off

The 350 S2 series

the line with just the right amount of revs – a fraction too much, and it wheelied; too little and it bogged down. The Mach II was also about 40lb heavier than the Avenger 350.

One thing that contemporary road testers of the era agreed upon was that the S2 drank petrol at the same alarming rate as the H1 500. Hard riding returned 19mpg on the motorway for *MCS* tester Dave Minton in '71, whilst *Bike* reported in '73 that the S2 returned an average of just 23mpg. *Popular Mechanics* in the USA claimed 28mpg average, about the best achieved by any of the press. Fuel capacity on the S2 is just 3.5 imperial gallons, with half a gallon held in reserve, so typical range was just 70 miles or so before the need to find a gas station.

The chassis of the S2 and S1 were essentially identical. A cradle type, steel tubular frame, closely based on the H1 design, holds the canted forwards motor, with a pair of Ceriani-style forks up front and three-way adjustable shocks at the back. The swing arm was shorter than on the H1, reducing the overall wheelbase from 55 inches to 52.5. Many riders in the '70s upgraded the swing arm bearings to the needle roller type, by the way, rather than the stock plain bearings. The UK-spec S2 ran 18 inch diameter wheels front and rear, with Yokohama tyres as OE equipment – wet weather grip was poor. Most testers praised the light, responsive handling of the S2, although, with hindsight, the S2 perhaps lacked the H1's violent, 60bhp kick in the pants that upset the chassis so much.

The 180mm front drum on the S2 was okay in its day, but cannot be recommended for modern day riding. It tended to fade under hard use and, like all drum brakes, requires regular maintenance to keep the 'feel' of the brake nice and progressive, rather than grabby. The S2's rear drum, like nearly all the Kawasaki triples, is spongy in operation.

One tiny detail on the S2, which seems ordinary nowadays, is that the new Kawasaki triple had its ignition key slot set between the clocks, instead of near the cylinder head, or buried somewhere unreachable on the frame. This was praised as real progress in '71, preventing ignition keys from vibrating loose and dropping onto the road.

Sidemm in France was arguably the keenest fan of the first Kawasaki S2 triples, and its founder, Xavier Maugendre, made the S2 the mainstay of his Coupe Kawasaki production race series for the 1972 season. The S2 arrived in France too late in '71 to replace the 350 Avenger twins in the Coupe Kawasaki series, but proved a popular model in '72 in that country. The Coupe Kawasaki series was linked with *Moto Revue* magazine, and so the S2 gained plenty of publicity, without Sidemm having to spend a fortune on advertising.

French market advertisement for the new S2.

350 S2 collector's notes

The very first '71 S2 models are the rarest and likely to have the highest values in the long term. Many dealers and importers in Europe found obtaining parts from Kawasaki in Japan almost impossible, the result of which was that complete bikes were unpacked from their crates and used as spare part donor machines. France, where the race series caused extensive damage to several bikes, and the UK, where Agrati was especially bad at providing spares back up to its dealers, are prime examples of markets where genuine, original, locally registered '72 bikes have all but disappeared.

For the '72 model year the reflectors at the front moved from the frame down tubes to the headlamp mounting brackets. For the S2A model the side reflectors moved yet again, to the top of the rear shock absorber and the fork legs. Collectors may find some parts have been retro-fitted to a '71-72 model, and the reflector positions can help identify this.

US-spec S2 models had a block tread pattern front tyre, which looked very similar to the rear Yokohama tyre. European S2s had a ribbed type. The grab-rail was changed from S2 to S2A models, and so the rail for the first S2 models is extremely hard to find as a spare part. Again, this is another component which can be missing from a '71/72 S2, along with details like the owner's handbook or the spare plug case under the seat.

1971-72 350 S2 spotter's guide

Sold as the 350 SS in Japan and as the Mach II in the USA market.

Same decals on fuel tank and tailpiece as '71/72 H2 750 and S1 250 models, featuring distinctive wavy stripes.

Pearl Candy Red was the only official colour for UK and French models.

Drum brakes front and back. Front drum has a black painted plate on left-hand side.

Seat has distinctive block pattern and high 'flip' at the tail, identical to S1 250 and H2 750.

All S2s had an optional grab strap across the seat; an optional handlebar mirror was offered as well.

Front mudguard painted same colour as fuel tank and side panels.

Many US models fitted with a short rear mudguard.

A total of 111 S2 350 models were officially imported to the UK during 1971, with 165 in 1972, according to Agrati Sales.

Some UK models had a vehicle registration plate mounted crossways above headlight, rather than 'cheesecutter' style on front mudguard.

A thicker, 19mm cylinder head was fitted to the S2 from engine number S2E07595. Early ones could crack, as they were 16mm thick.

Engine numbers: S2E00001 on.

Frame numbers: S2F00001 on.

The main markets for this model were the USA, Canada, and Japan. Limited numbers reached Western Europe and Australia.

350 S2A

Off the gas and hitting the brakes

1973 was the year that changed the automotive industry forever, as the Arab-Israeli war provoked a six-fold increase in the price of crude oil, then an embargo on exports by OPEC producers, which led to petrol rationing in many developed nations. Luxury and sports car makers went bust within months, and moped sales boomed in Europe as commuting costs rocketed and inflation caused a wave of strikes. A few months before this chaos unfolded, Kawasaki launched an updated range of two-stroke triples, with the 350 S2 now gaining new styling, seat, and a front disc brake.

Other details worth noting are the revised position of the indicators, with the rear set moved back slightly on the sub-frame. The S2A also had a new seat design which had a reduced 'flip' at the back end of the padded area, plus a new grab-rail and revamped tail section. Underneath the new seat the owner's manual was fastened securely inside a plastic pouch. The fuel tank changed, too, and now sported a locking fuel cap, which was handy, as petrol-siphoning became a national sport across the USA and Europe in '73.

Kawasaki didn't list any engine changes for the S2A, but it did have new exhausts, fitted primarily to meet US noise regulations set by the EPA. Peak power was a claimed 44bhp developed at 8000rpm, and Kawasaki also claimed a 13.6 quarter

The 350 S2 series

S-2 350

mile time. The reality was a sluggish 14.9 as tested by *Motorcycle World* magazine.

Kawasaki made slight changes to the port timing inside the motor to help it work more efficiently, and with the new, quieter exhausts. Well, that was the theory, but contemporary road testers reported average fuel consumption of 24mpg – even worse than the S2.

The S2A's front mudguard was a chromed steel item, not painted plastic. The instrument dials assembly was slightly different too, canted back towards the rider just a touch and featuring a raised top lip to the speedo and rev counter, which Kawasaki said was "to counter glare" in bright conditions.

The most obvious change was adoption of a front disc, a 277mm diameter item replacing the old-fashioned twin leading shoe drum. Road tests at the time praised the disc brake's predictable operation, but hated its squealing noises. This criticism must have stung Kawasaki a bit, as it had been fitting a new disc pad to eliminate squealing from the introduction of the S2A model.

A more serious problem affected all the triples; loosening of the oil pump backing plates, leading to leakage and then engine failure. The S2A series from June '73, or engine number SS2E41105, had a new banjo bolt gasket to try and prevent this happening.

Kawasaki used the disc brake opportunity to replace the forks with new alloy items, which obviously had a caliper mounting, but also featured new internals. The idea was to firm up handling a touch, though most reviewers of the era don't seem especially impressed, and it's arguably the back end which is the real weak area on the S series 350s. The S2A had new, five position, preload-adjustable rear shocks, but these were still too soft for sporting riders. It's no surprise that nearly every rider in the Coupe Kawasaki or KH400 race series threw away the stock rear shocks.

Blue and orange were the colours for the '73 Mach II 350.

73

THE KAWASAKI TRIPLES BIBLE

As the oil crisis deepened near the end of '73, interest in small engine motorcycles perked up in the USA.

This modified S2 was in action at Bikers Classic on the Spa circuit in 2009.

The S2A was strikingly different from the original S2 and, for some, is less beautiful. The lines across the gas tank and tail section were straighter, and the thin strip of metal tacked onto the side of the seat looked just that; a bit tacky. North American models still had side reflectors, by the way, but, for '73, these were located near the shock mounts and on the fork legs. There was also an optional mirror mounted on the left handlebar. The push-to-operate choke lever retained its position on the right-hand throttle assembly.

The S2A kept the same three coils, contact breaker points ignition, and 140w generator electrical system as its predecessor. Wheels remained 18-inchers, but the OE front tyre now featured a block

THE 350 S2 SERIES

pattern, unlike the '60s-style ribbed type on European S2 models.

The S2A was backed by a large advertising campaign in the USA, and most of the production run was sold there. Dealer Ed Moran recalls that his shop in New Jersey was able to sell 480-500 triples per year between 1971 and '73. Sales were weaker in Europe as Kawasaki hadn't got around to setting up subsidiary companies.

1973 350 S2A spotter's guide

The S2A model arrived in spring '73 in the UK; it's possible some '72-spec S2 bikes would have been registered on a '73 plate.
General restyle of the bike; front drum replaced by disc brake, new forks, bodywork, paintwork, fuel tank. Locking fuel cap.
New colour schemes were Candy Orange, Candy Blue and Candy Gold. Blue and orange were used for UK-spec S2A models.
New seat now had thin metal strip highlight on the side; no grab strap.
Tail section revised, S2A had a slightly different grab-rail.
Rear indicators fitted further back on seat sub-frame.
New 'dashboard' included cowled clocks, plus central warning light console.
New kick-start lever design.
US versions have side reflectors set on front forks and top of rear shocks.
Coloured front mudguard/fender replaced by chrome-plated item.
Engine numbers: S2E28226 on.
Frame numbers: S2T00001 on.
Markets: mainly USA, Canada, Japan, Western Europe, and Australia.

Most European market S2 models lacked the reflectors and raised handlebars of the USA and Canada Mach II machines. (Courtesy Triples Klinik Deutschland)

Visit Veloce on the web – www.veloce.co.uk / www.velocebooks.com
Details of all books in print • Special offers • New book news • Gift vouchers • Forum

CHAPTER SIX

THE 400 S SERIES

Davick Motique was the most go-ahead of all the UK Kawasaki dealers in the period '72-75, and actually had a demo fleet: almost unheard of in British motorcycle retailing back then.

Taking the 350 S2 out a few cubic inches, yet still utilising the same basic chassis for the 250 as the 400, wasn't technically difficult and saved money. In 1974, having a 400 capacity bike also marked out Kawasaki as different, as this was just before Honda launched its CB400F four and two years before the RD400 arrived. Being 'different' was an important consideration for Kawasaki then, part of establishing a unique identity, different to its Japanese rivals.

400 S3

Bigger engine, less performance

The 400 triple was introduced as the S3 across most western European markets in the summer of 1974, and it was immediately obvious that, beneath the universally admired styling changes, the new 400 was a softer, easier to ride bike than the 350 S2A.

The '74 S3 engine was based on the S2, featuring a four-bearing crankshaft (later, six-bearing on some S3 and S3As), horizontally split crankcases, steel cylinder liners, and 120 degree crank throw. The transfer ports had some rounding off work carried out on them, to both improve gas flow via revised port timing and ease workload on the piston rings.

Basically, Kawasaki's theory was that the 'softer' edge on the ports would make it less likely that the edges of the rings would 'push' into the port itself. By rounding off the port edges a touch, friction would be reduced and therefore piston ring life extended. The S3 had oil metered directly to its crankshaft main bearings and a splash feed via induction tracts for the upper cylinders.

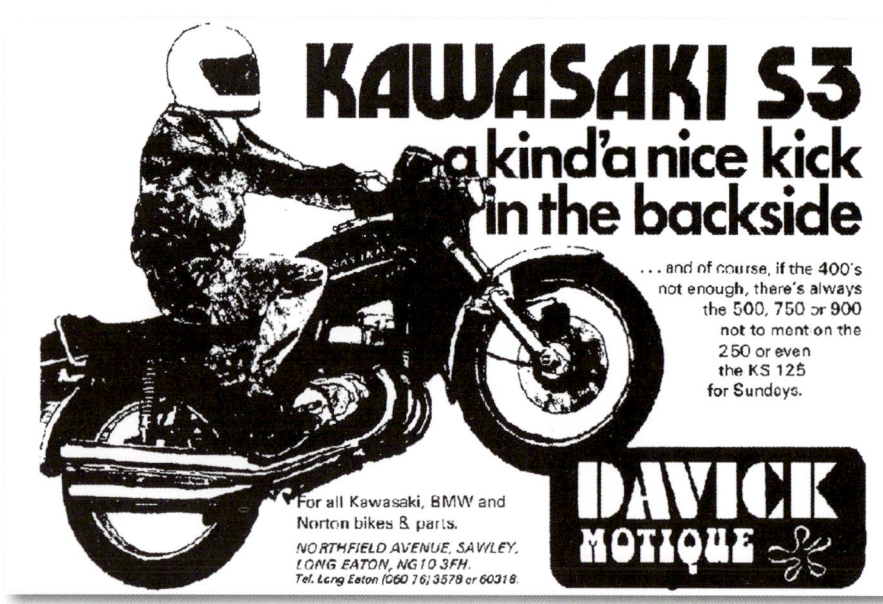

The 400 S series

Italian enthusiasts could buy the 400 S3, whereas the smaller 350 S2 had been subject to an import ban to protect local manufacturers of smaller capacity machines. (Courtesy Adolfo Drago)

Interestingly, the new S3 breathed in through 26mm-sized Mikuni carbs, increased 2mm in diameter from those fitted to the S2. If meeting the EPA emissions regulations and saving fuel really was top of Kawasaki's agenda, you would think that a mere 1mm increase in carb size would have done the job.

The motor was fairly low compression at 6.5:1, quite a bit lower than the S2 (7.3:1), and was of over square dimensions, with 57mm x 52.3mm bore and stroke measurements (same stroke as the 350 S2, but wider cylinder bore; exact capacity was 400.4cc).

This cubic capacity caused a problem in the UK market. Lee, from Doug Hacking Motorcycles in Lancashire, recalls that prospective buyers would get cold feet after receiving an insurance quote. "The insurance industry then was dominated by Norwich Union, which grouped bikes of 351cc to 499cc in the same bracket. So the S3 and KH400s cost more to insure than its main rival, the Yamaha RD350."

UK brochure for that year's range, including the 400 S3 model.

77

Claimed peak power was 42bhp at 7000rpm, a fairly modest rpm figure for a two-stroke at that time, and 3bhp down on the 350cc S2. The S2 made peak power at a claimed 8000rpm. By '74, the triples were being phased out by Kawasaki and deliberately softened all round. The S3 also had a rubber-mounted motor to reduce the vibration reaching the rider via the frame. Incidentally, a later modification to the wiring was made because the S3 suffered electrical gremlins, traced to a ground wire between the engine chain cover and the frame reacting to the rubber-bushed shaking action. A new wire was fitted from chassis number S3F0005187 during '74.

As regards fuel economy, Kawasaki did the job right on the S3. *Motorcycle Mechanics* reported that the S3 could average 37mpg in town, and 30mpg when giving the bike some stick on the open road. *Motorcycle Illustrated* recorded a 29mpg average, whilst *Cycle World* in the USA recorded 44mpg. These figures were much improved on the shocking 16-23mpg figures that the first S2 models managed.

The '74 S3 ran a conventional ignition, with coils and three sets of points. A permanent, magnet-type alternator was located on the same output shaft as the points assembly. The points required regular setting to keep the engine in peak tune. Early S3 models could blow their headlight bulbs, and later a lower voltage regulator was fitted to deal with the problem, applied from S3F0236 models, so quite early in the S3 production run.

Incidentally, although the UK S3 models had NGK grade nine plugs as standard specification from new, (NGK eights were fitted for running-in) UK dealer Davick Motique fitted Champion plugs back in '74, simply because it found the bike ran better.

The S3 ran a five speed gearbox with the ratios slightly altered from the 350 S2's spec. The difference was minimal, but the S3 is slower accelerating than the first S2 models as a result of this over-gearing. Fifth gear is almost overdrive on the 400 S3, it can be difficult to get the S3 to attain its theoretical top speed. On the upside, the S3 cruises better than the S2 above 70mph.

As if to partially acknowledge this fuel-saving, over-gearing wheeze, Kawasaki UK offered the 1975 S3A owner an optional 38- or even 41-tooth rear sprocket, instead of the stock 37-tooth item. This gave the 400 much needed kick-ass acceleration or wheelie potential for those who liked that kind of thing.

Primary drive was via straight-cut gear, taken from the right-hand end of the crank, with the S3 utilising a wet, six-plate clutch. All the 400 series transmissions can suffer problems from the nylon outer section of the clutch lifter – it can get chewed up and coated in chain lube as it's located right next to the gearbox sprocket. This makes things feel sloppy, and stripping the motor to get at it can be fiddly.

The 400 S3 also had the same splined adjustment linkage as the 350 S2 and S1 series, which is another well documented source of excess play and wear, and there's very little you can do to remedy this fault.

The steel tubular, cradle-type frame was very similar to the S2, with a longer swing arm stretching the overall wheelbase from 52.5 inches to 53.7 inches. Kawasaki also set the S3's fork angle at a leisurely 28 degrees, which was again aimed at making the bike feel stable. The frame had some reworking to its top rail section, with extra bracing near the headstock, and the S3 lost the friction-type steering damper.

The S3 was heavier than the S2, but nobody seemed to know by how much exactly. Some magazines listed it as being as light as 353lb dry, but *Motorcycle Mechanics* found it weighed 390lb wet, and *MCI* in the UK logged the S3 at a porky 402lb wet. That's some very heavy fuel and oil …

18-inch diameter wheels were fitted with Yokohama tyres as OE fitment. Brakes remained 10.9 inch disc at the front, with a drum at the rear. The rear brake also had a wear indicator fitted on the housing.

A new set of dials, warning lights and handlebar switchgear was introduced on the S3, too. The choke lever migrated to the left-hand handlebar, and an ignition kill

THE 400 S SERIES

switch appeared on the right-hand side. Lights were upgraded, although *Cycle World* noted that the rear lens cracked and fell off during the road test.

The S3 also came with twin mirrors as an optional extra in some markets, like the USA, for example. In the UK, twin mirrors were standard issue, some models retained the 'cheese cutter'-style front number plate, too. There was a brand new fuel tank design for the S3, which held 3.1 gallons and featured a slimmer locking cap.

is identical to the S3 model. It isn't clear when the switch from four to six bearings happened. Simon Lister, a lightweight triples specialist based in the UK, comments: "I have imported S3 models with both four and six bearing assemblies. Officially, the changeover comes with the introduction of the S3A model, but it seems Kawasaki made the change earlier and didn't list it in technical specs."

Kawasaki was still busy expanding at a rapid pace in '74 and '75. The new

400 S3 spotter's guide

The S3 model arrived in late 1974 in the UK: it's possible some '74-spec S3 bikes would have been registered as '75 models.

Candy Red and Candy Sky Blue were official paint schemes.

New, squared-off engine fins, rubber inserts added.

Seat has no thin metal strip highlight on the side, just grab strap.

S3 has a rounder-edged graphic on the side of the fuel tank, S3A 'boat prow'-style decal.

S3 has Mach II in small lettering on side panel, S3A does not.

S3 has choke lever on left-hand handlebar.

UK and Europe models had lower, flatter handlebars than North American market S3s.

Some UK-spec S3s fitted with 'cheese-cutter'-style front number plates.

Engine numbers: S3E00001 on.
Frame numbers: S3F00001 on.
Markets: mainly USA, Canada, Japan, Western Europe, and Australia.

USA-spec S3.

400 S3A

New bottle, same wine

The S3A for '75 was very similar to its predecessor. The main differences were cosmetic, with new graphics on the tank and tailpiece, new colours, plus the Mach II script disappeared from the side panels. A thin metal strip was added to the side of the seat, too.

Inside the engine the S3A had a six-bearing crank, but otherwise the motor

400s, two- and four-stroke, were part of a bigger marketing push. Kawasaki UK and Canada were set up in 1974, and the Lincoln Nebraska plant opened in the USA. The following year saw KMSA (South Africa) and Kawasaki Australia established also. According to Kawasaki's official literature, the S3A and KH400 were not sold in Africa, but others remember differently: "I recall buying one of the S3A 400s new, it was a dark red colour," says Chris Speight from KMSA, "as I was a big fan of the triples.

THE KAWASAKI TRIPLES BIBLE

Also, Kawasaki bikes had been imported to South Africa in small batches from the late '60s, but obviously numbers increased from 1975 once our company was set up."

Kawasaki also started its West German subsidiary in '75, replacing arrangements with Detlev Louis, and it seems that the S3 wasn't imported in great numbers. Louis was reportedly allowed to choose which early triples he imported. The later KH400 of '76 was a restricted 36bhp model, aimed at the favourable German lower power insurance grouping – many more of these would have been sold in Germany than the S3 series, as the S3 cost the same to insure as a H1 there.

400 S3A spotter's guide
The S3A model arrived in early 1975 in most markets. Candy Green and Candy Super Red were official paint schemes, though brown was available, too.
Seat has thin metal strip highlight on the side.
S3A has a sharper-edged graphic on the side of the fuel tank.
No Mach II in small lettering on side panel.
UK and European models had lower, flatter handlebars than North American market S3A models.
Engine numbers: S3E14300 on.
Frame numbers: S3F14300 on.
Markets: mainly USA, Canada, Japan, Western Europe, and Australia.

The 400 S3A model was available in brown, although Kawasaki did not officially list this colour option.

CHAPTER SEVEN

KH400 SERIES

The KH400 series was launched in January '76 in major markets like the USA, UK and France. The bike was similar to the S3, but Kawasaki had added CDI ignition and detuned the 400 slightly to meet US-led emission limits. Both motorcycle noise and 'dirty' smog-emitting vehicles were being targeted by the National

1976 KH400 for the US market in Dark Green. (Courtesy Lee Doxey)

Left-hand switchgear had the push-to-operate choke. (Courtesy D&K Motorcycles)

Highways Transport Administration and the Environmental Protection Agencies in the USA. As this was far and away Kawasaki's biggest market at the time, it had to take that political pressure seriously.

1976 KH400 A3

Smoothing the edges

As 1976 loomed, Kawasaki was moving away from two-stroke motorcycles, at least as far as its street model range went. The company had recently launched the 400cc and 750cc four-stroke twins, which had proved a hit in the USA. The Nebraska-built KZ400 was the top selling Kawasaki in the entire range in 1975. The triples' days were numbered.

Principal engine tuning changes for the KH400 A3 (there were no A1 or A2 KH 400 models) included a re-designed airbox, and extra steel mesh inside the exhaust baffles. The jetting changed inside the carbs, and the KH400 was one of the first two-strokes designed to run on unleaded, low octane fuel. These noise and emissions tweaks took 4bhp from the claimed output of the old S3A, dropping peak power from 42bhp to 38bhp at 7000rpm for the '76 KH400.

CDI ignition was a major step forward for the KH400, and it worked very well. New sparkplug caps were also fitted to make the bike run better in wet weather, and were partially successful. On the gearbox output shaft, the KH400 ran a 15-tooth small sprocket, rather than the 14-tooth item on the S3 series, thus raising gearing slightly. Acceleration over the quarter mile was no longer the main selling point of the mid-sized triple. There was a tweak to the clutch lever housing to try and make the action smoother, too. The KH400 had an upgrade to its electrics, with a new, three fuse box located under the seat. It was becoming a civilised, almost semi-touring type of motorcycle.

The frame received extra gusseting around the steering head, and the sub-frame near the shock mounts was strengthened.

KH400 SERIES

Softer springs were added to both the forks and the shocks. Most testers at the time praised the smoothness of the ride, although they noted the trade-off was a wallowy feeling when cornering hard.

There was a new, smaller, nine inch disc brake at the front end, with a one-piece caliper, featuring harder disc pads. Kawasaki claimed at the time that the new pads helped wet weather braking performance: they did, just, but anyone riding a KH400 today with the original brakes would probably carry a ship's anchor as back-up …

New colours for the USA market included Brown, Dark Green, and Candy Red whilst European KH400 A3 models came in Dark Green and Orange. The graphics on the petrol tank and tail section now featured distinctive yellow pinstripes, and new 'KH400' badges were fixed onto the side panels. For rider comfort the handlebars were rubber-mounted.

Group road tests in the USA often put the KH400 near the bottom, criticising its soft suspension, still greedy thirst, and lack of seating comfort. One magazine mentioned that the much-vaunted CDI ignition unit had failed on test. The model was quietly dropped from US and Canadian markets at the end of '76.

Above and next page: The KH400 was tested by Cycle *in '76 and the news wasn't good. (Courtesy Lee Doxey)*

83

The Kawasaki Triples Bible

Reception was better in the UK and Europe. In Germany, a special 36bhp edition was produced, purely to meet the unique insurance grouping which affected the West German market at that time. In the UK, *Bike* magazine found the KH400 "beautifully smooth" and "sophisticated," and posted a top speed of 100.3mph flat out. But the hard truth was that the KH was slower than the opposition from Honda, Yamaha and Suzuki, and the two winners in the 400 class in '76 were the CB400F and RD400. They outsold the KH400 by a hefty margin, and UK dealers began to discount the KH400 from 1977.

In France, Kawasaki Japan took a financial stake in Sidemm and began to market its bikes more aggressively, although, in the case of the KH400, the *Moto Revue*-backed Coupe Kawasaki series created excellent demand for the bike. Initiatives such as a helmet sponsor making a 'Samurai' rider of the meeting award at each round really got younger French riders

KH400 SERIES

fired up. At the start of 1976, over 300 entrants applied for Coupe Kawasaki, and many bought a brand new bike on which to try their luck.

1977 KH400 A4

The KH400 struggled on with Candy Emerald Green and Candy Royal Purple offered as colour schemes for '77 across Europe for the A4 model. The bike had a new, thinner pin striping motif on the tank and tail section and looked superb. Mechanically, it was unchanged; Kawasaki had pretty much lost interest by this stage and, apart from in markets such as France, the A4 was a hard machine to sell.

The triples were dropped from the USA altogether for '77, with Europe and Australia becoming the main markets after Japan. Some were sold in South Africa, too. The KH400 was a decent mid-range bike, but it had lost its performance edge. Compared to sales of the smaller KH250, the 400 struggled, especially in the UK. The crux of the problem here was that the KH400 was virtually identical to the KH250, barely any faster and, apart from its electronic ignition, offered little to warrant the extra £80 on the purchase price, or the running costs, one of which was expensive insurance. The KH400 went over the Norwich Union 350cc limit and NU then underwrote something like 65 per cent of the entire motorcycle insurance market.

Officially, Kawasaki Japan ceased

Above and next page: The A4 model in Candy Royal Purple, on show at the 2009 NEC Classic Motor Show.

85

THE KAWASAKI TRIPLES BIBLE

Right: The UK brochure for the KH400A4 in Candy Emerald Green, arguably one of its nicest paint schemes.

production at the end of '77, but if that's true then the factory kept itself busy by dreaming up new paintwork schemes for the KH400 until 1980. As regards the UK market, however, the '77 A4 models do seem to have been the last of the line imported by KMUK. All the photographs made available by Tony Jakeman, organiser of the KH400 race series in '79 and '80, do not show any A5 models in later colours. Also, the author bought a 'brand new' KH400 in the spring of '79, which was actually a '77 machine in Candy Purple. And no, I didn't get a discount off the list price either…

86

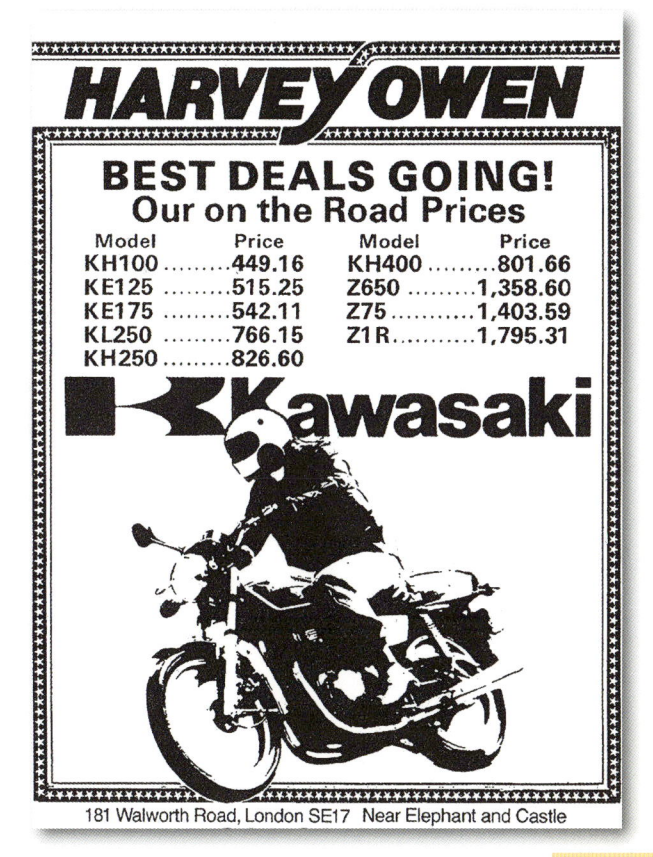

KH400 SERIES

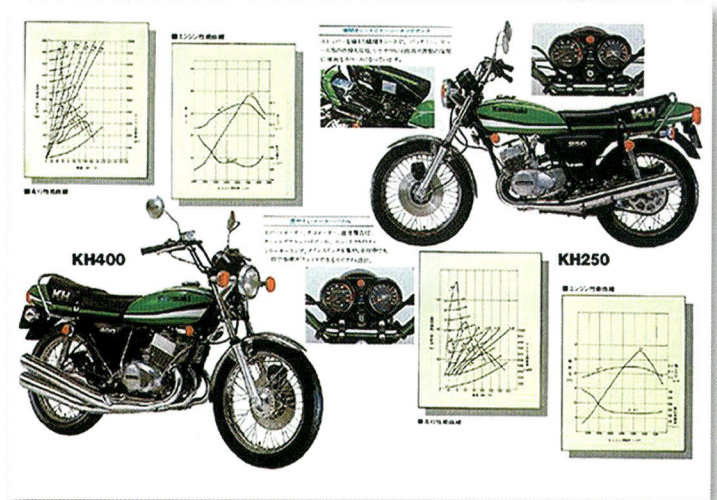

Above: The '79 KH400 got the same paint scheme as the 250 in Japan.

Left: By 1978, dealers were beginning to sell the KH400 more cheaply than the KH250 in order to shift remaining stocks.

The Japan-only KH400, with the same black side panels as the 250, probably sold during '79 and '80 as the bike was phased out.

1978 KH400 A5

The A5 was officially the final incarnation of the KH400, available in Candy Lime Green and Candy Persimmon Red. The '78 machine had a reworked seat, with the thin strip of metal trim vanishing from the sides. A new master cylinder was added to the handlebar assembly, too. It was virtually identical to the KH250 of the same year and had the same 'swoosh'-type decals on the fuel tank. According to both German and Italian triples enthusiasts, this was the final year for the KH400 in West Germany and most of Europe.

The final KH400 A5 models were listed in both '79 and '80 brochures back in Japan, however, featuring some interesting new colours. It seems likely that only very small numbers were exported; certainly none came to Europe. It is a reasonable bet to assume that some Ballington replica 250 and 400s went to South Africa.

Despite Kawasaki UK's attempt at boosting spare parts sales via the KH400 race series, backed by *Motorcycling Monthly* magazine, the model could only be sold by discounting the price in '79 and '80. The Coupe Kawasaki race series in France also switched to the Z650 fours around the same time.

Collector's notes
Because of insurance rules in West Germany, a special low power, restricted KH400 A3-A5 series was also available, making just 36bhp. The last of the '77 A4 models took up to

87

five years to sell in the UK market, so many will show a later registration plate.

In terms of rarity, the Japan-only models from '79 and '80 are likely to appreciate in value.

Total production of KH400 machines appears to be in the 18,000-20,000 range, the majority of bikes being A3 and A4 models.

For collectors it is handy that many parts are interchangeable throughout the run, and often common to the KH250 as well.

The seats are different from '78 on.

KH400 A3-A5 spotter's guide

The KH400 A3 model arrived in November 1975 in the USA for testing and evaluation; a few may have that year's registration.

Colours
A3: Dark Green, Orange, Candy Red. and Brown
A4: Candy Emerald Green, Candy Royal Purple
A5: Candy Persimmon Red, Candy Lime Green
The A5 also came in the Kork Ballington replika green and white, plus an unknown blue for Japan.

Seat has thin metal strip highlight on the side on A3-A4, but not A5.
Different pinstripes on the side of the fuel tank and tailpieces each year.
KH400 badge on side panel, except for Ballington replica.
Chromed front mudguard on all KH400s, not painted.

UK and European models had lower, flatter handlebars than North American or some Japanese market models. OE equipment twin mirrors on Euro models.
Engine numbers: S3E26300 on.
Frame numbers: S3F26200 on.
Markets: mainly Japan, Western Europe, and Australia. Sold in USA for '76 only.

CHAPTER EIGHT

THE 250 S SERIES

Top: US brochure pic for the '72 S1 features lower European handlebars and no side reflectors.

Bottom: The brochure made the 250's motor look as big as possible.

The S series 250cc triples were the longest running of them all, for one good reason: they offered a unique and thrilling ride for learner motorcyclists in the '70s. True, the S1 was a fast model, but it was downhill all the way from there in terms of performance, whilst Suzuki and Yamaha eclipsed the 250 Kawasaki by the mid '70s. But the little quarter-litre triple had great style, and a buzz saw sound which teenage riders loved. If you dreamed of owning the Mach III or H2 750, but had only an apprentice's wage, you bought a 250 Kawasaki because it was a stylish echo of its bigger brothers.

250 S1

White noise

The S1, also called the Mach I in the North American market, began production in Japan in March '71, according to Kawasaki's official history, launched later that year across the USA, and then the rest of the world in early '72. The two listed colours were Pearl White and Pearl Candy Red. Most of the European S1 models for '72 appear to have been white, with the red bikes offered in Japan and possibly North America. The Japan model was listed there as the 250SS.

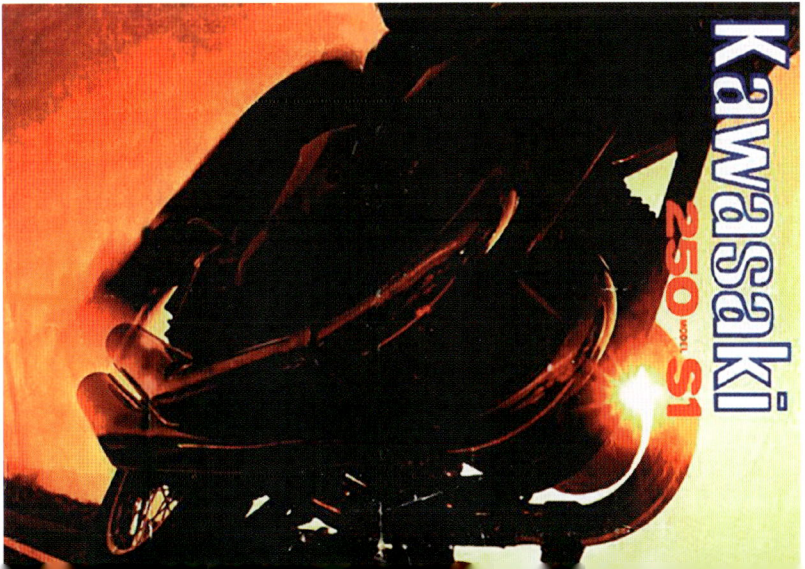

The S1 didn't feature in the 'Year of the Tri-Stars' advertising campaign in the US market for '72, but was on sale – just. It seems that relatively few '72-spec S1s made it into America, the main focus being the 350 S2 that autumn, and impending launch of the H2 750. USA correspondents at the Tokyo Show in late autumn '71 reported that they didn't think the new 250 would arrive in America until Kawasaki had received a favourable reaction to the 350 S2, launched in the USA in September '71. Kawasaki was quick off the mark, however, and it appears that some S1 models were registered in North America, Japan, and Australia. Numbers were probably in the hundreds rather than thousands. Small street bikes were – and still are – a tough sell in the USA.

When the S1 arrived in Europe during the spring of '72, the small bike was a bit of a hit. Back then, 250cc class machines were regarded differently in Europe, where a highly competitive 250cc road racing class attracted plenty of spectators, and various rules on motorcycle licences and insurance brackets created good demand for a 250 class machine. Key markets for the S1 were the UK, France, and West Germany. None were officially imported to Italy, since there was a law forbidding importation of sub-350cc machines at that time, although it would be naive to imagine that no Italian dealers sourced bikes from elsewhere.

Britain was a good market for the S1, and official figures from Agrati Sales are that some 330 S1 models were sold in '72. Some decent marketing would have easily sold twice that number ... The 250cc class was a fairly big part of the 76,000 unit market that year, as 17-year old riders in Britain could use a 250cc machine on L-plates, without taking any type of test. In markets like West Germany, steeper insurance costs for over 36bhp bikes meant that the 32bhp S1 was a relatively cheap bike for younger riders to own.

The S1 was well-liked by road testers. In the UK, *Bike* magazine reported that the S1 had the ability to cruise at 90mph on the motorway, although noted that UK dealer Davick Motique (UK importer Agrati didn't loan bikes to the press generally) had raised the gearing with a 16-tooth gearbox sprocket (standard was 14-tooth to help the S1 get nearer the magical 100mph top speed. A best of 98mph was recorded – tantalisingly close. Peak power was claimed to be 32bhp at 8500rpm, but later Kawasaki factory literature lists output for the S1 as 28bhp, which is more likely.

Technically, the S1 was very similar to the S2. The frame, bodywork, wheelbase, brakes – just about everything – were identical to the bigger machine. Apart from the barrels and pistons, there's very little to separate the two smaller S series bikes of '72. Using the 350 chassis made the 250 S1 heavy at 328lb, but saved on manufacturing costs, and arguably helped it feel stable for a 250, a more 'grown up' type of bike for a learner rider.

Other cost-cutting measures included three sets of points and three coils, rather than electronic ignition, plus the front brake didn't illuminate the rear brake light – only the rear drum did that. Both the UK- and German-spec S1 had lower handlebars than the Japanese and American models, plus they came with a grab strap across the seat. The US S1s also generally came without a rear mudguard, whereas the European models did – unless it rusted away.

Early S1 models could break their clutch cables, so a Teflon-coated, tougher cable

This restored S1 was on show at the National Exhibition Centre (NEC), UK, in 2009.

THE 250 S SERIES

was fitted from engine number S1E08257. The cable is 2.5mm thick, rather than the 2mm of the first S1 bikes, which can also suffer regulator failure. From 1973, a lower voltage unit was fitted.

In general, the S1 was well made, and it's fair to say that the primary reason so few have survived is down to the typical (young) age of the original buyer, and the resulting high chances of a crash/neglect sending the S1 to the scrapyard before its time.

1972 250 S1 spotter's guide

Colours were Pearl White and Pearl Candy Red.
Front mudguard is painted, not chromed.
UK and European models had lower, flatter handlebars than North American models.
Like the 350, S2 rear brake has matt black backing plate.
Original bike came with tool roll in tailpiece.
Mirrors were optional extras.
Many UK-spec bikes featured a front number plate.
Chainguard should have a series of round holes in it, same as S2.
Engine numbers: S1E00001 on
Frame numbers: S1F00001 on
Markets: mainly USA, Canada, Japan, Western Europe, and Australia.

S1A

Boxing clever

In line with the bigger 350 and 750 triples, the 250 S1A for 1973 received a styling makeover, with new colours being Candy Orange, Candy Blue, and Candy Gold. The front fender was changed to a chromed item, and there was a new seat to match the re-shaped tail section, with a smaller tail light. The seat wasn't quite as long, so if you got lucky at the disco your chick would have to squeeze that bit closer ...

Whilst the essentially similar 350 S2A received a front disc brake for the '73 model year, the little 250 kept the 180mm drum. This may have been a budget decision, but the S1A had new exhaust internals, plus some changes to the ports and carbs to try and make the bike cleaner and quieter. It is debatable whether this robbed the S1A of significant power, but even 2-3bhp means a great deal to a 250. A leading US magazine tested the bike and recorded a leisurely 16 second quarter mile time. Not too exciting ...

The S1A also had a new set of dials and a more modern dashboard assembly, with a central console housing the ignition key and 'idiot' lights. The new seat had a helmet lock, there was a sight window in the oil tank, and a locking fuel cap. The choke lever moved to the left handlebar, so you couldn't ride off with the choke held on. The S1 was becoming a civilised first bike, even if it had lost some of its fire. Yet Kawasaki still sold the triple on its performance credentials, at least its US advertising copywriter did, claiming a "genuine 100mph" top speed and 14.7 second quarter mile. More realistic figures would be low 16 seconds for the quarter mile and 90mph top speed.

A Japanese ad for the new 250 S1 and 350 S2 depicts them as touring machines.

91

THE KAWASAKI TRIPLES BIBLE

Candy Red US-spec S1A. Note the side reflectors for the North American market.

S-1 250

1973 250 S1A spotter's guide

Colours: Candy Orange, Candy Blue, Candy Gold.
Seat has thin metal strip highlight on the side.
New shorter seat, revised tailpiece.
Chromed front mudguard, not painted.
UK and European models had lower, flatter handlebars than North American models.
Engine numbers: S1E05494 onwards.
Frame numbers: S1F04691 onwards.
Markets: mainly USA, Canada, Japan, Western Europe, and Australia. UK official numbers were 300 units.

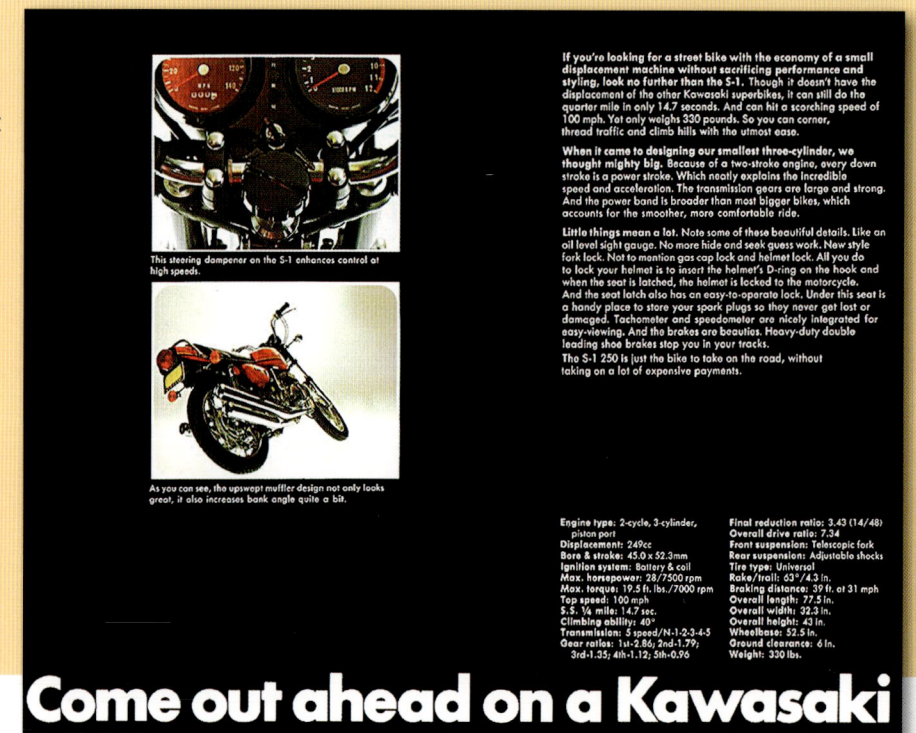

This steering dampener on the S-1 enhances control at high speeds.

As you can see, the upswept muffler design not only looks great, it also increases bank angle quite a bit.

If you're looking for a street bike with the economy of a small displacement machine without sacrificing performance and styling, look no further than the S-1. Though it doesn't have the displacement of the other Kawasaki superbikes, it can still do the quarter mile in only 14.7 seconds. And can hit a scorching speed of 100 mph. Yet only weighs 330 pounds. So you can corner, thread traffic and climb hills with the utmost ease.

When it came to designing our smallest three-cylinder, we thought mighty big. Because of a two-stroke engine, every down stroke is a power stroke. Which neatly explains the incredible speed and acceleration. The transmission gears are large and strong. And the power band is broader than most bigger bikes, which accounts for the smoother, more comfortable ride.

Little things mean a lot. Note some of these beautiful details. Like an oil level sight gauge. No more hide and seek guess work. New style fork lock. Not to mention gas cap lock and helmet lock. All you do to lock your helmet is to insert the helmet's D-ring on the hook and when the seat is latched, the helmet is locked to the motorcycle. And the seat latch also has an easy-to-operate lock. Under this seat is a handy place to store your spark plugs so they never get lost or damaged. Tachometer and speedometer are nicely integrated for easy-viewing. And the brakes are beauties. Heavy-duty double leading shoe brakes stop you in your tracks.

The S-1 250 is just the bike to take on the road, without taking on a lot of expensive payments.

Engine type: 2-cycle, 3-cylinder, piston port
Displacement: 249cc
Bore & stroke: 45.0 x 52.3mm
Ignition system: Battery & coil
Max. horsepower: 28/7500 rpm
Max. torque: 19.5 ft. lbs./7000 rpm
Top speed: 100 mph
S.S. ¼ mile: 14.7 sec.
Climbing ability: 40°
Transmission: 5 speed/N-1-2-3-4-5
Gear ratios: 1st-2.86; 2nd-1.79; 3rd-1.35; 4th-1.12; 5th-0.96
Final reduction ratio: 3.43 (14/48)
Overall drive ratio: 7.34
Front suspension: Telescopic fork
Rear suspension: Adjustable shocks
Tire type: Universal
Rake/trail: 63°/4.3 in.
Braking distance: 39 ft. at 31 mph
Overall length: 77.5 in.
Overall width: 32.3 in.
Overall height: 43 in.
Wheelbase: 52.5 in.
Ground clearance: 6 in.
Weight: 330 lbs.

Come out ahead on a Kawasaki

S1B

Pocket green meanie

Another series of changes to the look and feel of the 250 occurred for '74, even though the basic chassis and engine combination remained the same. Paint choice was just the one: Candy Green, possibly one of the most collectable colours for the little S series 250s. Again, the seat was changed

92

THE 250 S SERIES

1974 250 S1B spotter's guide
Colours: Candy Green only
New seat loses 'flip' at the end, no side strip.
Brake lining wear indicator on rear drum.
New gas tank and different cap.
Chromed front mudguard, not painted.
No steering damper.
'Mach I' in small letters on side panels of USA models.
UK and European models had lower, flatter handlebars than North American models.
Engine numbers: S1E12001 on.
Frame numbers: S1F12001 on.
Markets: mainly USA, Canada, Japan, Western Europe, and Australia. UK numbers were 300 units officially.

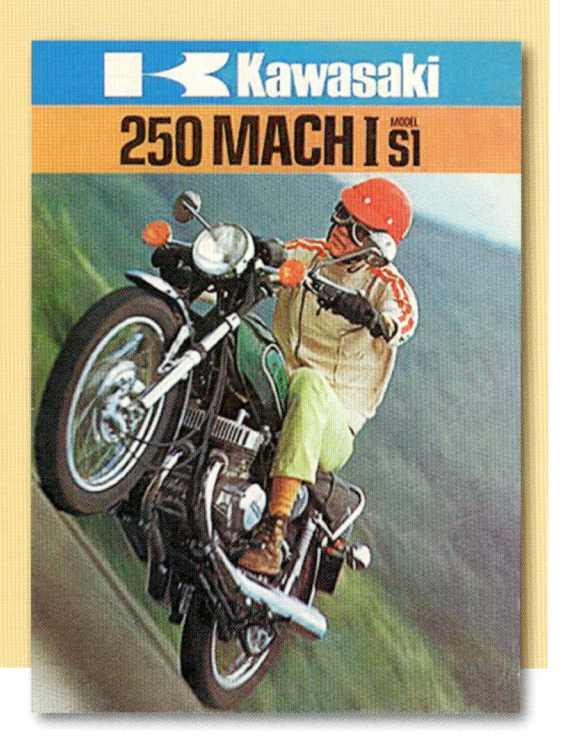

Brochure for the 74 S1B for the Australian market.

along with the tailpiece. The S1B lost the friction steering damper, and was fitted with new shocks, which were claimed to give a firmer ride.

After the initial excitement of the 'Tri-Star' launch for '72, Kawasaki got cold feet about the US market at the end of the following year, making drastic cutbacks in its road racing budget for '74. The emphasis had very definitely switched to four-strokes, now that the Z1 had been acclaimed the superbike 'King,' and a range of Z400/750/200 four-strokes was in the pipeline.

In the triples range, launch of the new 400 S3 put the old 250 very much in the background with the US motorcycle press. It was a machine better suited to Europe's growing number of teenage novice riders, and Kawasaki began to step up promotion of the S1B in France, West Germany, Scandinavia, and the Low Countries. Britain still had Agrati to contend with until Kawasaki UK officially opened for business in the autumn, so the official Agrati figure of 300 S1B units sold must be considered with a dash of scepticism.

1975 250 S1C

Baby Blue
The '75 S1C was one of the top selling Kawasaki triples in the UK market for two reasons. Firstly, the 250 class enjoyed a huge jump in sales generally, so demand increased sharply and, secondly, Kawasaki had set up its own UK subsidiary in '74, improving the dealer network spares supply, and advertising heavily in the UK motorcycle press – the first time that the Kawasaki name had really been seen in the same professional way as Honda, Yamaha and Suzuki sold their products. Kawasaki UK introduced a range of clothing, chain lube, and other branded accessories to complement its bikes; there was even a crankshaft exchange service on the triples for those who forgot to top up their oil tank and melted their main bearings.

This was all driven by Kawasaki Japan, of course, which had seen huge rises in sales figures in the USA and other markets in the space of a few years. It had also opened a manufacturing plant in Nebraska, and a centralised spares distribution, dealer and

93

THE KAWASAKI TRIPLES BIBLE

This S1C isn't quite right; the Halibut Blue colour is a respray, but it does have the holder with three spare plugs under the seat, however – always handy.

warranty support centre near Amsterdam in Holland.

The UK market in '74 and '75 was booming, despite the recession, strikes, and power cuts, etc. The two-wheeler market in the UK had grown from 85,000 units in '69, when the H1 was launched, to 189,000 units in '74, Some 40,000 of those new sales each year were 250cc bikes, and Kawasaki wanted a bigger slice of that than the feeble 300-350 250 S1 units Agrati could shift.

Two senior executives from Japan had

THE 250 S SERIES

spent eight or nine months negotiating terms with UK dealers, planning ad campaigns, a road race team led by Stan Shenton, an off-road squad headed by Alex Wright, and putting a proper press office and test bike fleet in place. John Norman had been poached from BMW GB and was working with senior Japanese staff, holding 'secret' meetings in the Holiday Inn, Hyde Park, throughout most of '74 before formally launching the UK operation.

"I knew John Norman well from his days

> *"The machine of the year"
> is only the beginning
>
> # Kawasaki Motors (UK) Ltd. has been established to give you a better deal
>
> We have created a new company, Kawasaki Motors (UK) Ltd., to be the sole distributor for Kawasaki motorcycles and spare parts in this country. It will also be responsible for supervising after sales service systems in order to give all Kawasaki owners the best possible support through a specialised Dealer Network.
>
> This new organization is dedicated to uphold the good reputation Kawasaki motorcycles enjoy in many countries around the world. A reputation for engineering excellence, outstanding performance and remarkable reliability. They are motorcycles that deserve the best of factory support after the sale and Kawasaki owners can now be confident of the full backing of Kawasaki Heavy Industries Ltd., one of the largest industrial groups in the world, and Europe's latest computerised parts centre Kawasaki Motors N.V. This is a commitment to existing and prospective owners that will be respected and honoured.
>
> *Yours sincerely,*
> KAWASAKI MOTORS (UK) LTD.
>
> **Kawasaki**
>
> **Kawasaki Motors (UK) Ltd.
> Telephone: Staines 51444**
>
> ** The Sporting Press of America, Italy, France & U.K.*

Kawasaki spent heavily promoting its new UK regime. "Machine of The Year," by the way, was the '73 Z1.

with Honda," recalls Cheshire dealer Bill Smith, who had been a pioneer Kawasaki dealer in the '60s, "and he was the guy who transformed Kawasaki UK in my opinion. Some of the dealers Agrati had appointed were too small, or had three other franchises. Kawasaki was growing up, getting professional. The downside was it focussed on the four-strokes from then on; the triples were finished after the oil crisis, basically."

At a glance the S1C hadn't changed much for '75, apart from its colour scheme of Halibut Blue and the usual seat variations: some S1Cs have a metal strip on the side, some don't. Also, some models have shock absorbers with a polished alloy shroud at the top (the reflector is positioned there on

The 250 S series

Engine bottom end of the S1 series is tough; top end a little more prone to wear and tear.

US models), whilst some had a conventional plain spring over the damper rod. One final detail worth noting is that the '250' badges on the side panels changed to a white script that stands out, which makes it easy to spot an S1C with incorrect panels.

According to Kawasaki, the S1C developed 28bhp at 7500rpm as did all its predecessors, except the original S1 of '72. It seems more likely that Kawasaki made the same efforts to get the smallest triple to emit less smoke and noise as it did with the bigger triples between 1972 and 1975.

There's a good reason for reaching this conclusion: the S1 series remained officially listed in the US range through to the end; indeed, the KH250 models were sold there in '76 before Kawasaki USA finally threw in the towel with the 250 two-strokes in America. Changes to exhaust baffles, airbox, air filters, and carb settings seem highly likely, even if not listed in official literature at the time.

UK road testers found that the S1C could hit only 87-89mph, around 10mph down on the S1 of '72. On the upside, it used less fuel, returning nearly 40mpg when ridden gently; around 30mpg when thrashed. The bike had mysteriously put on some serious weight, now weighing in at 368lb wet, according to *Bike* magazine, whereas the S1 was a slim 328lb. An increase of 40lb is astonishing, if the magazine figures are correct, and does partially explain the reduced performance of the S1C.

The Kawasaki Triples Bible

1971-75 250 S1-S1B-SlC collector's notes

There's no doubt that the very earliest 1971 S1 models will be the most collectable in the long run, simply on the grounds of rarity. Most of the production run – around 4400 units – seems to have been sold in the USA but, compared to the bigger triples, the Mach I, as it was known in North America, wasn't a big seller. Maybe 3-400 examples were genuinely registered before January 1st 1972, which was the official 'model year' for the Mach I. It's possible another 1200-1500 S1s then hit America and Canada in '72. Few now remain intact, and many were drastically modified over the years. Some were even raced.

The next most collectable would probably be the 1973 S1A from Europe, again, due to the relatively low numbers sold and the even fewer survivors. The styling was never that popular, making the A series unloved for probably the best part of two decades. Many were scrapped.

There was a handful of racing S1 250s in the USA, mainly drag race machines in the '71 and '72 seasons according to US triples enthusiasts. Only three or four riders attempted to race the essentially production S1 in open class 250 road racing. One of this small number is in a private collection in the USA; nobody knows if the other few survived.

The last of the S series 250s, the S1C, was a handsome, well-equipped and competitive machine in its day. Substantial numbers were sold in the UK, West Germany, France, Australia, and Japan, and that makes it the most practical proposition in terms of collecting, restoring and sourcing spares to keep it on the road. Be warned, however: restoring a 250 triple costs much the same in time and money as a bigger model, but it will never be worth anywhere near as much as the big 500 and 750 Kawasaki triples.

1975 250 S1C spotter's guide

Colours: Halibut Blue only.
Seat can have thin metal strip on the side, or not. Both are correct OE fitment.
Grab strap fitted on European models, not on US ones.
Chromed front mudguard, not painted.
UK and European models had usual lower, flatter handlebars than North American models.
UK models came with one mirror, left-hand one was an optional extra.
Tool kit in seat hump, strap retained it.
Seat had owner's manual beneath and a sticker featuring a diagram of oil tank location.
Engine numbers: S1E17100 on.
Frame numbers: S1F16300 on.

Visit Veloce on the web – www.veloce.co.uk / www.velocebooks.com
Details of all books in print • Special offers • New book news • Gift vouchers • Forum

CHAPTER NINE

KH250 SERIES 1976-81

The KH250 outlived all its bigger brothers, staying in production until the late '70s in Japan, and then proving hard to sell in various dealerships around the world as first the Suzuki X7, then the Yamaha RD250LC effectively became the only 250 sports models that young riders really aspired to own. Both the Suzuki and Yamaha handled better, posted a genuine 100mph top speed, and looked sleeker, much more modern than the decidedly '70s-style KH opposition.

In the UK market, dealers tried cutting the price of the KH250 by as much as 25 per cent and desperation set in as the 1982 licence law – which would restrict learner riders to 125cc class bikes – loomed, thus rendering nearly all the 250 machines practically unsaleable overnight. It was a sad end to what had been the *MCN* 250cc 'Machine of the Year' just a few years previously.

1976 KH250 A5

Halfway house

The KH250 A5 was a stopgap model, rather like the mythical H1C. It featured a drum front brake, and best estimates as regards total production are somewhere in the 1500-1800 region. The A5 was then superseded by the B1.

The A5 had many features in common with the B1 and was delivered late in '75 to North America and Europe. It seems likely that the A5 didn't arrive in the UK; certainly, no contemporary road tests of the time mention any models between the last of the S1Cs tested in summer '75 and arrival of the B1 in January '76.

But it was sold in West Germany, according to Kawasaki club enthusiasts, plus Holland and Italy in small numbers. It appears that Kawasaki deliberately held back from truly 'launching' the A5, as the B1 model with new forks, disc brake and other changes, was already on its way for January '76.

The only colour scheme for the A5 was Candy Super Red, and it had three pinstripes on the gas tank and tailpiece, just like the B1. There was a complete upgrade of the electrical system on the A5 model, featuring three, colour-coded circuits, each with its own fuse.

For whatever reason, Kawasaki had decided to keep plugging away with the street triples in 250cc and 400cc in the USA for '76, despite the runaway success of the Z400 twin in the novice/commuter end of the market. To meet California emissions and noise regulations, Kawasaki stifled the US-spec A5 with a more restrictive inlet

THE KAWASAKI TRIPLES BIBLE

Triple treat: high-spirited sprinters with sm[ooth] 3-cylinder 2-stroke engines and

KH500

KH500. New gears for the road racer's street machine

You're looking at the latest edition of the original superbike we introduced in 1968. We've improved it every year. Now it's well-mannered and easier to ride with a wider performance range in every gear because we've given it more torque. But it's still the quickest 500 off the line and safer with its new gear shift pattern 1-N-2-3-4-5, just like our other machines.

This year we also added a brighter headlamp (12V 45/40W), a locking fuel cap, new fuse set-up, a more comfortable seat, improved rear suspension units, positive engine stop switch and larger mirrors.

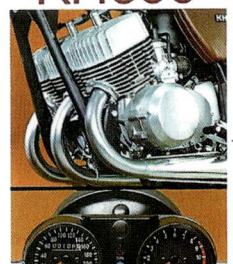

Kawasaki built a reputation for performance and reliability on this machine. The KH500 has come of age. It delivers 52 hp at 7,000 rpm and can get your adrenalin going even if you're a road racer. The more you know about motorcycles and if a sprinter is your style, this is the only machine for you.

KH400

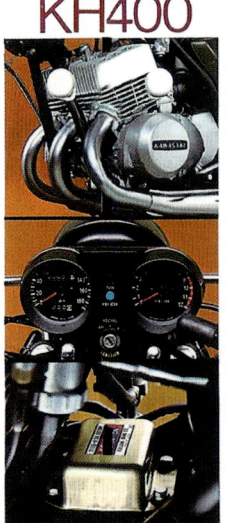

KH400. More horses for your money and a new CDI system

You can do a lot with 38 hp at 7,000 rpm at the twist of the wrist. You can streak ahead of the traffic and into the country for a weekend with your girl riding with you. All the power you need is there. So are the comforts.

The KH400 is better than ever. We gave the 3-cylinder 2-stroke engine a whole new set of sparks from a space-age Capacitive Discharge Ignition (CDI) system that lights the fires and is more reliable.

And the new locking fuel tank, separate fuse system, larger mirrors, improved shocks, re-designed seat, and engine stop switch make this machine a lot easier to live with. You'll like the way the power comes on, the extra reserve of power in every gear and the way the machine handles. The frame is the same race-proven double cradle that's hard to beat. The disc in front and the drum rear brake are a combination to keep you confident. All the equipment is there: big speedometer and matching tachometer, hooks for two helmets, 5-speeds and a style that stays fresh.

The KH250 B1 was aimed at the 'Young Man About Town' by Kawasaki USA in 1976.

100

KH250 SERIES 1976-81

ooth, sophisticated disc brakes

KH250

The world's only 250 cc triple gets a disc

One of a kind! Ride the only 250 3-cylinder 2-stroke because it delivers the smoothest power. It's a sophisticated lightweight with all the advantages of a multi. It's made for the kind of rider who knows and loves a beautifully engineered machine but doesn't have to prove anything. He only want's the best in the class.

This is Kawasaki's smallest triple but it's built just like its bigger brothers. What's new this year?

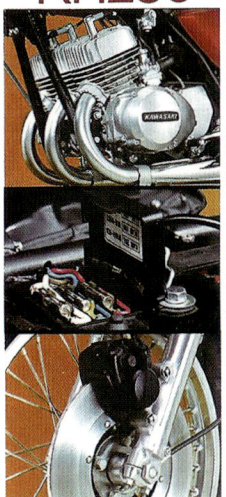

It has a new disc brake in front, neat styling, a new fuel tank lock, separate fuse system, larger rear vision mirrors, a more comfortable seat, better rear shocks and positive-action engine kill switch.

This is the bike for the Young Man About Town who likes nothing better than to take to the hills when he has a chance and feel the thrill of motorcycling in a burst of speed and safe handling that clears the cobwebs and sharpens the reflexes. It's a luxury you can afford.

tract, so the engine couldn't breathe as well. Quoted power remained as 28bhp at 7500rpm officially, but it's hard to see how the engine could be made less efficient and yet the power remain the same.

1975-6 KH250 A5 spotter's guide

Colours: Candy Super Red only.
Chromed front mudguard, not painted.
UK and some European models had lower, flatter handlebars than North American models. Some Italian models had raised 'bars.
New electrical system can be identified by new fuse box under seat.
Drum front brake and forks from S1C model.
Engine numbers: S1E026600 on.
Frame numbers: S1F24400 on.

1976 KH250 B1

The endless summer

Arrival of the KH250 B1 in '76 coincided with one of the boom years for 250cc class machine sales across Europe, as that summer saw an incredible six-week long heat wave across much of Europe which did much to promote sales of motorcycles of all sizes.

In the UK, Kawasaki gave the new B1 variant a real push, getting road test coverage in all the main magazines and offering the bike as a competition prize, too. The 250 class was especially competitive that year with the Suzuki GT250A model and the first 'coffin-tank' or speed block-styled RD250 from Yamaha on offer. The KH250 was the slowest

101

The Kawasaki Triples Bible

in a three-way *Which Bike?* test, posting an 89mph top speed against the 95mph set by its two rivals. *Bike,* meanwhile, found that the new Kawasaki was smoother and better braked than the crude Moto Guzzi 250-TS, but no faster. Interestingly, the test machine loaned to *Bike* magazine that year was painted Deep Burgundy, the same shade as the '76 KH500 for that year, though this was not an official Kawasaki colour for the smaller KH250. I's possible that Davick Motique had the bike painted, but Kawasaki may have produced a few in this scheme to gauge dealer reaction to the new model in late '75.

Bob Goddard from *Motorcycle Mechanics* magazine in the UK could coax only 86mph from the B1, and noted that as well as the new front end, the B1 also had revised shocks and extra gusseting to the frame: it shared its chassis with the KH400 for that year, by the way. For the very first time in the UK market the 250 triple came with twin mirrors as standard, even if rear view was pretty restricted. The main change to the KH250 B1 was the addition of the 11 inch front disc, which was hailed as a major advance at the time. The new front forks were made of alloy, rather than steel. OE tyre fitment was Yokohama in the UK, by the way, on 18 inch wheels front and rear. 1976 retail price was £539.

In West Germany Detlev Louis' independent Kawasaki import operation had now been replaced by a wholly owned subsidiary, and the KH250 was marketed for the novice rider. According to German triples clubs enthusiasts, the colour schemes were identical to UK-spec models, and lacked the raised handlebars and side reflectors of US and Japanese models. Sales of the KH250 in France were outshone somewhat by the success of the 400, which had the massively popular Coupe Kawasaki race series to help promote sales.

In the USA the KH250 B1 took its place alongside the 500 and 400 triples, all now using the KH model identification, rather than the old 'Mach' suffix. It was the final year for the two-stroke triples in the US market, and Kawasaki USA's attention was concentrated on the KH400 and KH500 rather than the small 250.

According to Kawasaki's official information, a California version was made which claimed 26bhp at 7000rpm, rather than the stock 28bhp output. It's hard to know exactly what changes were made, but carb and air intake restrictions seem likely, if meeting EPA clean air regulations was the aim. As far as I can make out, no B1 models were road tested by the US motorcycle press, and advertising appears non-existent. The KH250 was offered in the same colours as European models: Candy Super Red, which actually looked orange, and Candy Sky Blue, which was actually closer to a Royal Blue 'in the metal.'

Gary Bonella on his KH250B1, with Janet, in the late '70s. The large luggage rack was a typical accessory of the time.

1976 KH250 B1 spotter's guide
Colours: Candy Super Red, Candy Sky Blue, with three pinstripe decals.
Chromed front mudguard.
UK and some European models had lower, flatter handlebars than North American models. Some Italian models had raised 'bars.
Disc front brake and new forks, master cylinder on right-hand handlebar.
Engine numbers: S1E028801 on.
Frame numbers: KH250B 000001 on.

1977 KH250 B2

The slowest triple
1977 was a bad year for the KH250.

102

KH250 SERIES 1976-81

It appears that the attempt to keep the bike alive in the US market led to the 26bhp version of the KH250 being foisted onto the rest of the world. Kawasaki went four-stroke only with the street model line-up for '77, but the KH250 and KH400 continued production in Japan, with Europe, Japan, and Australasia being key markets. Some seem to have been sold in South Africa, too, though numbers were small.

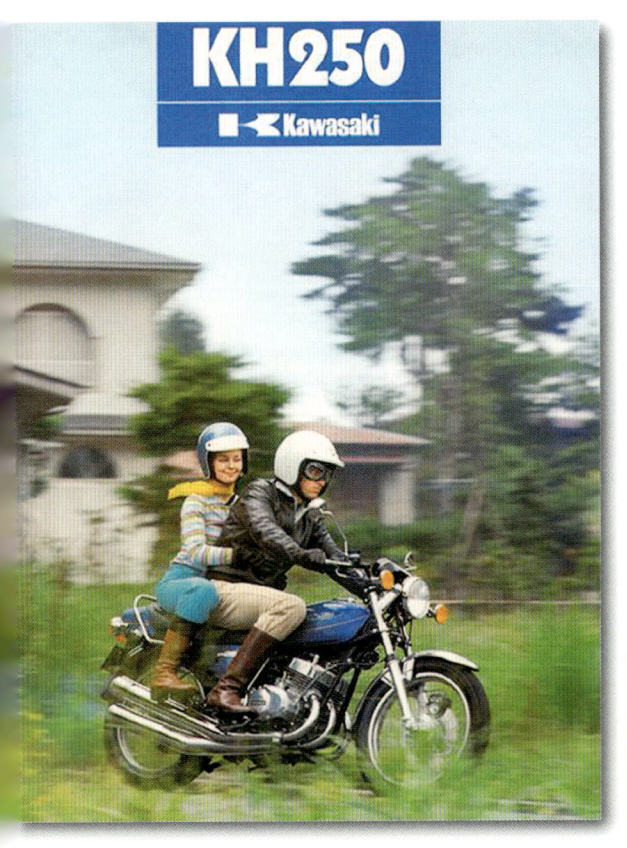

In the UK the KH250 was still being trounced by the Suzuki GT250, the top selling 250cc machine of '76, helped by an ad campaign headed by Barry Sheene, then World 500cc Champion. The Suzuki GT250B model for '77 was less peaky than its predecessor and, alongside the RD250, continued to damage sales of the KH250. The B2 model had a new paint scheme, of course, with Candy Wine Red and Candy Orient Blue the official colours.

The restricted power was down to airbox revisions on the B2 model, which effectively strangled the bike at the top end of its power curve. It retained the same low gearing as its predecessors, so accelerated reasonably well, but simply ran out of steam at speed. The author's brother bought a B2 brand new in April '77 and spent hours removing and drilling the exhaust baffles, messing with the carbs, and removing the air filter unit to try and crack an indicated 90mph top speed. It was hopeless; in fact, the bike went slower. The only time he ever saw a speed above 90mph was downhill towards the Creg at the Isle of Man, with the engine revving beyond 10,000rpm.

In stock trim the B2 model could reach an indicated 85-87mph flat on the gas tank (probably about 80mph, in reality) and was seen off by the two-stroke opposition from Yamaha and Suzuki. On the upside, it was faster than Honda's plodding CJ250 and, unlike the Benelli 250C, the KH250 had an electrical system that worked when it rained, except for the plug caps. Fuel consumption averaged about 30mpg ridden hard and, as the B2 had no real pull below 5000rpm, hard riding was required.

The B2 goes down in history as the slowest triple ever made, and is unloved by collectors today. Still a great looking bike, though.

The B2 in Candy Wine Red.

1977 KH250 B2 spotter's guide
Colours: Candy Wine Red and Candy Orient Blue.
One thin pinstripe on fuel tank and tail piece.
No North American models.
New left-hand switchgear assembly.
Engine numbers: S1E038401 on.
Frame numbers: KH250B008601 on.

103

THE KAWASAKI TRIPLES BIBLE

1978-81 KH250 B3-B5

The final flourish

Visually, the last generation of KH250 models were essentially identical to the B3 except for colour changes. The engine made a claimed 28bhp once again, although this time peak power output was developed at 7000rpm, rather than 7500rpm, according to Kawasaki. Quoted top speed was around 90mph, but this seemed tame compared to machines like the Suzuki X7 and Yamaha RD250LC which came along and finished

Gary Bonella's cousin, Paul, on his B3 back in 1978.

A UK-spec B3 in unrestored condition.

KH250 SERIES 1976-81

off a glorious era of novice riders thrashing around the roads on two-strokes.

In the UK, the motorcycle market peaked in 1980-81, with new sales of around 300,000 units, incredible for a recessionary period. Within that 300K pie there was a slice of about 65,000-75,000 250 class sales to be fought over, which was one good reason why Kawasaki kept making the 250. In Japan there were stricter rules regarding the licence arrangements for younger riders, so 250cc and 400cc machines sold in large numbers then.

The '78 KH250 B3 came in Candy Lime Green or Candy Cobalt Blue, with the green especially popular in the UK. Gary Bonella in the UK owned a red B1 model in '78, whilst his cousin bought a B3 in Lime Green: "The KH250s we had were regularly seen off by Yamaha and Suzuki machines – I remember the KH250 was about 5-10mph slower – but ours looked and sounded better."

Whilst Kawasaki worked on the Z250

Top: A Japanese model B3, but with high 'bars and reflectors typical of US market triples. By 1978, none of the triples was exported to America.

Above: A Candy Lime Green B3 model. (Courtesy Abergavenny Motorcycles)

105

The Kawasaki Triples Bible

Scorpion four-stroke, the B3 and B4 kept the brand in the vital 250cc class. The B3 received a few tweaks: the seat was changed slightly, supposedly to make it more comfortable two-up, and the master cylinder changed from the simple twist-on type to one which required a screwdriver to remove.

For the B4 model only the colours changed, with a block pattern on the fuel tank: you could have a lime green model, with white block, or vice versa. The bike was still thirsty; Johnny Doome in the UK runs a B4 model today, and says "fuel consumption can be as low as 17-18mpg, but the bike howls at high revs. It's handy to lay down a smoke screen when being followed by the police, too ..."

The new, but rather dull, Z250C

KH250 SERIES 1976-81

arrived in 1980, selling alongside the B5, which was the very last of the line. This has the distinctive KH logo on the seat and a simple '250' badge on the matt black side panel. The paintwork was inspired by Kork Ballington's GP-winning machine, although that bore no resemblance to the air-cooled triple in any way. Incidentally, a KH400 with exactly the same paintwork was sold in Japan but never made it to Europe.

By this time, the KH250 was outclassed by newer 250 bikes, and when the UK government announced in 1981 that learners would be restricted to 125cc machines with no more than 12bhp, the bottom fell out of the 250 market. Gary Bonella recalls those days. "Dealers couldn't sell them, you could get hundreds off the official 900 quid list price. My cousin realised that his KH was almost worthless when he tried to part exchange it, so he kept it – we restored it in 2002 and that became addictive: I now own ten triples!"

Some dealers tried to shift remaining stocks by cutting as much as 50 per cent off the price, whilst others offered a KH250 free if a rider bought a Z1300 new, which was another Kawasaki flop of the late '70s.

Lee, from Doug Hacking Kawasaki in Lancashire, remembers they were patient. "We knew they would sell eventually, I think we were registering both the KH250 and KH400 machines up to three years after production ceased in 1980, so a '79 model might have an X registered '81 plate on it."

Many other UK and European dealers simply stored the smaller triples in a back room or outbuilding, often in their packing cases. Enthusiasts also found caches of 250 spares in many dealerships which sold up later in the '80s and '90s. The KH250 B series still makes a fun Sunday ride today, and, for many riders, remains inextricably linked to their teenage years.

Opposite page:

Top: Johnny Doome's B4 shows the change to matt black side panels. (Courtesy Johnny Doome)

Main: The KH250 B4 model.

Above: Japanese brochure for the B5, the last of the KH250 models, and the two-stroke triples.

107

THE KAWASAKI TRIPLES BIBLE

> **1978-80 KH250 B3-B4-B5 spotter's guide**
>
> Colours:
> B3: Candy Lime Green, Candy Cobalt Blue.
> B4: White with Lime Green block, or Lime Green with White block.
> B5: Ballington team green colours, white and green.
>
> B5 has KH on seat, 250 badge on side panels.
> Identical Japanese market KH400 Ballington replica in '80.
> B3 model:
> Engine numbers: S1E048301 on.
> Frame numbers: KH250B -018501 on.

A UK market brochure for the B4 model.

KH250 series 1976-81

Collector's notes

It's probably fair to say that the last of the line will prove the most collectable eventually. They were poor sellers in 1980, and that may make them rare one day, even if some dealers did hold onto uncrated, brand new examples. The seats featuring the 'KH' logo will also be in short supply at some point in the future, making them valuable items.

Otherwise the Candy Lime Green B3 of '78 would seem to typify the era and the model range itself. It allegedly returned to full 28bhp specification, finished in a classic Kawasaki paint scheme, and sold in healthy numbers, so parts supply looks reasonably good, too. The B4 model in red was quite a rarity; most featured the two-tone white/green paint scheme.

Best estimates on total KH250 production would be in the 28,000-30,000 range from 1976-80, so there are still fairly plentiful numbers around. Values will never rise to dizzy heights; if you look at the historic values of, say, British machines in the 250cc bracket, you can see how the market nearly always rates bigger motorcycles as better long term investments.

Below and following page: The Dyson Originals and other bodywork kit specials might one day be worth investing in due to their rarity.

109

The really rare KH250 machines are the UK specials like the Dyson and FLF body-kitted bikes, yet their future value is unpredictable. Flow Line Fabrications and Ian Dyson Originals were two of the more successful aftermarket kit makers in the 1970s, and the smaller 250s were sometimes customised with the flowing, almost Vetter-inspired panels, plus expansion chambers – usually Micron or Allspeed. From a collector's point of view, bodywork condition and insistence on a lime green colour are possibly the main considerations when buying a Dyson or FLF.

The KH250 series was supposed to suffer gearbox faults, but triples specialist Simon Lister thinks much of that is apocryphal. "The riders were novices, of course they missed, or crunched, through gears. The selector mechanism is tough, the whole engine is really. Only attempts at tuning the 250s damaged them seriously. Fitting an electronic ignition is one way of making a KH250 more user-friendly now."

CHAPTER TEN

The racers

On the track, Kawasaki needed to prove its performance credentials by winning more than a few drag races in California. The groundwork was laid with the A1R and A7R twins, plus the V4 125cc water-cooled machine which Dave Simmonds used to clinch the '69 World 125cc Championship.

As regards the triples, the H1R came first, then the H2R – an altogether more serious proposition. Both FIM GP 500 and F750 glory eluded Kawasaki, but both bikes were potential race winners. From '69 on, the green and white colour scheme became synonymous with Kawasaki, too, eventually becoming the more vibrant 'Team Green' under the directorship of Bob Hansen, and later adopted as the official factory colours for almost all motorcycle competition.

Bill Smith on the H1R racer, featuring twin fuel tanks, which finished 3rd in the Senior TT at the Isle of Man in 1970. (Courtesy Bill Smith)

111

H1R 500

The clubman's grand prix winner

It is remarkable that, within 15 months of the road-going H1 500 being launched in 1968, a kitted factory race version was made available to privateers in the USA and Europe. But then Kawasaki was also quick to introduce race variants of the A1 and A7 twins soon after the road models appeared: it was a company in a big hurry to make its mark on the track.

Given the amount of work needed to develop both the 500 Blue Streak and 750 New York Steak road bikes between 1964 and 1968, Kawasaki did well to create an H1R privateer race machine, with nearly all the development work completed in the USA utilising the H1 500 in various road races. The H1R was a decent machine from the start; in fact, with Kiwi racer Ginger Molloy onboard, the H1R put up a respectable challenge to the dominant MV Agusta 500 fours in the triple's debut 1970 season. Christian Ravel in France took a win straight-from-the-crate with the H1R at Le Mans that year.

The challenge to the dominant MV Agustas wasn't before time, as 500cc GP road racing was a dull procession in 1968-69. Honda pulled out in '67, so the only rivals MV Agusta had in the 500 class were arthritic British singles and twins, or the odd home-brewed special, like Ginger Molloy's Bultaco 360 two-stroke, for example. Spectators at long circuits like the Nürburgring could brew a cup of tea waiting for someone to appear once Ago had sped past in the lead.

Tweaking the original H1

Long before Kawasaki had the first batch of factory H1Rs ready in late '69, keen privateers were already modifying the road-based H1 500 bikes in that year's road racing season, mainly trying their luck by entering it in some big prize money, one-off races.

UK motorcycle dealer/importer Bill Smith rode an H1 racer, put together by Reads (London-based Kawasaki importer), at the North West 200 in May '69. This public road race, held in Northern Ireland, was a real test for a two-stroke, with long straights where a race machine was flat out for minutes at a time. The H1 500 impressed spectators and paddock pundits alike with its sheer speed, but, almost inevitably, seized its engine whilst Smithy was in the lead with just a few laps remaining.

Was it tuned? Bill Smith says not. " We never touched the engines as we figured Kawasaki knew far more than we did about building big two-strokes," recalled Smithy in 2009, "but all the two-strokes seized back then: Bultaco singles, Suzuki and Yamaha twins, Jawas, the lot. It was something you expected in a race."

Another Reads of London unmodified H1 was campaigned at Thruxton, also in May '69, by Tony Dunnell and Bill Penney. The bike was entered in the 'Thruxton 500' production class motorcycle race, which, interestingly, banned any production bikes with DOHC four-stroke, or disc valve induction two-stroke engines. Odd rules, you might think, perhaps favouring the makers of old pushrod British twins, but it gets better: the organisers also allowed the Triumph-BSA factories to enter 'production' Bonnevilles and 650 Lightning twins, which they brought along especially for factory test riders like Percy Tait.

Unsurprisingly, the race was won easily by Percy Tait and Malcolm Uphill on a Triumph 650 Bonneville with the ill-handling H1 down in 23rd place, failing to keep pace with 250 Suzuki and Ducati bikes over the 500 bumpy miles around Thruxton. *Motorcycle Sport* magazine reported at the time that Penney and Dunnell were "grimly trying to get used to the wallowy handling and violent acceleration of the 500." *MCS* went on to note that the seven inches of travel in the H1 500's forks made cornering "difficult."

Remarkably, Dunnell and Penney raced the 500 Kawasaki wearing OE Japanese Dunlop K77 tyres, which – as anyone who has ridden on early Japanese tyres from the '60s and '70s will know – was a gutsy thing to do on any track, never mind Thruxton's wildly undulating surface.

THE RACERS

If the reader can imagine how Tony Dunnell felt after wrestling the 500 Kawasaki around Thruxton, put yourself in his boots as he lined up at the top of Bray Hill for the 500 class Production TT race just a few weeks later. On the upside, the TT rules were less restrictive than those applied to UK mainland road racing, so the Read's of London H1 500 had a fairing, race seat, and, most importantly of all, tweaks to the suspension to make the 500 H1 more stable on the scary Isle of Man public roads course.

Dunnell was able to fly past the speed trap at the Highlander pub at 118.4mph on his opening lap. Indeed, he looked set for a famous victory on the H1 500, with a 66 second lead in the 500cc class on the final lap. But, on his final assault of the Mountain section, Dunnell crashed at the very fast 33rd Milestone corner. The bike was wrecked and Dunnell was knocked out as he cartwheeled through a fence. There's no margin for error on the Island, then or now.

The Read's team cited the wide engine on the Kawasaki 500 H1 as the cause of the crash, and told *MCS* that the crankcases dug in as Dunnell took the 33rd Milestone. This seems likely, as several early attempts at racing the H1 featured dodges and tweaks to raise the motor in the frame, both to increase ground clearance and route the pipes beneath the engine, instead of alongside it. A look at the later 'slimline' crankcases of the H1A 500 does suggest it was an inherent design flaw in early H1 500s which made them a bit of a bastard to corner.

London-born racer Reg Pridmore, who later went on to successfully race BMW boxer twins in the USA, tried fitting an H1 motor inside a Norton featherbed frame for a race at Brands Hatch in '69. Reg was arguably the first man to put the Kawa triple into the famous Rex McCandless tubework, but it didn't pay off. For reasons unknown, Pridmore withdrew from the race after struggling in practice.

There was some success in '69 for the upstart H1 500, though. Most famously, Christian Ravel won the 1000km race at Le Mans on the Sidemm-Tebec-sponsored H1, which ran an oversized fuel tank, Ace 'bars, and had its lights removed – otherwise virtually stock. It was surprising that a two-stroke triple could last in endurance races, but it did well sometimes; a trio of tweaked 500 H1s took 2nd, 3rd and 4th at the Bol d'Or 24 hour endurance race held at Le Mans in '69, just beaten by a CB750 Honda. There was also a notable race victory in a 6 hour endurance race at Zandvoort, with Spahn and Noorlander riding a modified 500 road machine.

But what the road-based 500 H1 couldn't quite do in '69 was win a GP race against the top teams and riders of the day. However, Kawasaki was feverishly working in the USA to improve the 'production' H1 500 race machine and, by the late autumn, had ready the basis of the H1R.

So, despite the patchy results for the road-based H1 race machines, there was genuine excitement amongst privateers when the H1R appeared in December '69, with orders invited for the 1970 race season from dealer-backed teams, or selected riders. The H1R had a claimed 75bhp, weighed less than an MV Agusta, and was cheap for a factory race machine, at a reasonable £1500 in the UK.

The official H1R in clubman trim, as offered by Kawasaki to privateer racers.

The H1R at the TT races

"It handled like a turd in a piss-pot"
When the H1R appeared in the winter of '69, Bill Smith bought one for the 1970 TT races. Smithy's H1R also had some extra

113

modifications from its factory specification, especially for the TT course.

"We knew the 500 engine drank fuel from the '69 North West," recalls Bill, "plus, the bike handled like a turd in a piss-pot, so doing well in the Senior TT was going to be difficult. We left the engine in standard tune. It was fast enough, but if we had tuned it the thing would probably have drank even more fuel. The problem regarding fuel consumption was very serious, because I needed to complete three laps before a pit stop. We worked out during practice on the island that we were using three gallons on a single 37 mile lap. We solved the problem by having twin gas tanks, a seven gallon main one, with a three gallon reserve tank built into the seat unit."

Push-starting the race with ten gallons of petrol on the bike wasn't easy, but Bill managed it. "The weight of the bike was incredible, it was a really heavy bastard to push off the line. I took off down Bray Hill, held on for grim death and wondered if it would stop at Quarter Bridge."

The drama didn't end with a wobbly opening run down Bray Hill with over 60lb of fuel on board, as the clutch packed in on lap two, and as Bill hacked the Kawasaki through its gears trying to catch Jack Findlay in 2nd place, he noticed the handling of the H1R got decidedly worse on the final lap. "I thought there was oil or fuel on the back tyre, it was all over the bloody place on the last lap. When I stopped, the team checked the rear wheel and found it had just nine spokes left from thirty-six. All the bumps and jumps around the island had just about done in the wheel – it was on the verge of collapse."

Despite this shaky Senior TT debut, Bill's verdict on the H1R racer was that it was a generally strong race machine, with a very tough engine, plus excellent brakes.

"The general opinion now is that the front brake wasn't up to much." noted Bill in 2009. "Many replaced it with a Fontana unit. I didn't think it was bad at the time. In fact, the front drum on the first H1R 500 was a copy of a Fontana twin shoe, and, as copies go, it was good enough for 3rd at the TT."

As the 1970 season went on, however, it became apparent that the real weakness of the bike as a GP 500 racer was its raging thirst. "The high consumption meant you had to keep stopping," says Bill, "races were longer then, so the H1R rider had to stop more often. Also, it never quite came together as a good handling bike – the engine sat too high in the chassis."

Although they'd just taken 3rd at the IOM Senior TT in '70, and had a range of 750, 350 and 250 road bikes in the pipeline, Kawasaki had other projects to consider. Bill remembers another detail which told him a great deal about Kawasaki's long term planning. "After the 1970 TT was over, I gave a senior Kawasaki director a lift to the Renolds chain factory in Manchester because he told me they were planning a 1000cc, four cylinder road bike. They wanted a guarantee from Renolds that if the British firm supplied the Z1's OE chain, it wouldn't break. Renolds couldn't give them that guarantee, so they used a Japanese chain supplier instead.

"I was pals with Bob Hansen in the USA then and he let slip that Kawasaki was asking him to get as many technical details on the Honda CB750 as possible before he left Honda and joined Kawasaki's race team, which had always planned to race four-strokes in the long term, no matter how successful the triples might have been."

The European development riders

You would have expected Kawasaki to back its only GP champion, after Dave Simmonds won the 125 World Championship for Kawasaki in 1969, in the blue riband 500cc class, but the company didn't give Dave a works contract for the 500cc GP Championship in 1970. With hindsight, it appears baffling, but Kawasaki then was 100 per cent intent on the US market, and didn't want to invest a fortune in chasing European GP glory when the clear target was the USA.

Instead, Simmonds got a privateer machine and was left to make the best of

Dave Simmonds' H1R race machine, restored and on display on the Isle of Man.

it – much like his 125 GP effort, in fact, which continued alongside his 500cc campaign in 1970. The H1R didn't handle well, so Simmonds had a special Reynolds frame constructed by Ken Sprayson.

Dave Simmonds' brother-in-law, sidecar racer Mick Boddice, recalls the first time Dave rode the H1R. "He just took it up the road for 10 minutes to get the feel of it, and came back looking white-faced. He said something like, 'I can't ride that thing on the Island, it'll kill me.' Then he phoned Ken Sprayson."

Dave struggled to get near the podium in 1970 and subsequent seasons. A typical race in 1970 was the East German GP at the Sachsenring, where Simmonds made a halfway decent 8th place. In the same event Martin Carney posted a 3rd place, utilising a bigger fuel tank to minimise the number of fuel stops. Dave could see that he'd have to do some work to be competitive in '71, so fitted a six speed gearbox to the engine and, more importantly, had Ken Sprayson fabricate a frame from Reynolds tubework and fit Girling shocks to improve handling. Kawasaki offered a hopped-up H1RA race machine for '71, but Simmonds worked with what he had. The reason was simple; he couldn't afford to buy the new H1RA and begin extensively modifying its chassis, on the off chance that the newer model would be a better bike than his current project.

Simmonds' H1R was promising. In fact, Kawasaki probably would have gladly taken the Sprayson-framed machine in part-exchange for an H1RA, and learned a great deal from it. But corporate pride probably ruled that out. Dave's bike had interesting details, such as a cutaway fairing lower which placed the exhaust pipes out in the cooling breeze, not tucked behind the fairing as on the stock H1R. The dry clutch had its own cut-out panel in the fairing, too.

The large, eight-gallon fuel tank, with a deep rear section, really made the most of available space around Sprayson's beautifully precise frame tubes. The frame allowed the engine to sit further forward, too, improving handling. Simmonds was also a rider who had criticised Kawasaki's choice of gear ratios, right from A1R days, so his six speed 'box was a personal solution to getting the power down at a variety of corners on European GP circuits, where

The Kawasaki Triples Bible

A restored H1R in 2009 at the Stafford Classic Mechanics Show.

everything from 1st gear hairpins to 140mph sweepers could test bike and rider. The H1R's five speeds might have been okay on US speed bowls, but the European GP tracks were an eclectic mix of adapted street and newer short circuits.

All these technical changes – which represented patient, thoughtful machine development and featured absolutely no input from Kawasaki – worked well. Everything came together in Spain, where Dave Simmonds posted Kawasaki's first-ever 500cc GP win at Jarama in the '71 season.

Again, you might think Kawasaki would have backed Simmonds with a factory GP team in '72, but no, Dave was essentially a 'Continental Circus' privateer for his final season. He did acquire an H1R-A-spec motor, however, for 1972, which proved to be his most successful 500cc class season, although a 2nd place was his highest GP finish.

In October that year, however, Simmonds died whilst trying to put out a caravan fire at a French circuit, and racing lost one of its best development riders. Dave's modified H1R was sold to Sven-Olaf Gunnarsson (minus the engine, which Mick Boddice put in a sidecar racer), who competed on it in the 500 GP season in '73. The bike was later exhibited by Kawasaki UK at the Centenary TT races in 2007.

Thunder from down under

Ginger Molloy had the most success in the '70 GP season, with a 2nd place overall in the 1970 Grand Prix 500cc Championship on his H1R. Although Molloy didn't replace the frame on his bike, he was, like Simmonds, a

THE RACERS

patient and resourceful GP rider working on a tight budget, and he tweaked the H1R's electrical system, worked on the porting inside the motor, and made a host of gradual improvements as the season went on.

Ginger started well with a 7th place at Daytona on a brand new, straight-from-the-crate H1R, totally unmodified, though it was obvious from his first races that fuel consumption was too high, which cost race places. After getting 2nd place at Le Mans, Molloy followed Bill Smith's idea and converted the tailpiece to a second fuel tank, relocating the oil tank to a lower position under the seat.

The next race saw a split breather pipe throw fuel all over bike and rider, plus the extra weight made handling worse. Molloy fitted a wider rear wheel rim to try and calm the H1R's pig-on-roller-skates handling.

After repairing his own worn crankshaft main bearings (because Kawasaki couldn't/wouldn't supply spares), porting the engine and fitting a Krober ignition, it all came together with a 2nd place in Finland and another 2nd in Ulster. Victories in Austria and Yugoslavia, plus another couple of podiums late in the season, showed that the bike was a winner – once various faults had been ironed out.

Finally, after all the promise shown by Degner's MZ racers, followed by the screaming little Suzuki, Tohatsu and Yamaha bikes in the early '60s, the two-stroke racer looked set to eclipse the four-stroke in Grand Prix competition. Riders and public alike could sense the balance of power shifting towards the smoky strokers.

Gregg Hansford is possibly the most famous Aussie to race the Kawasaki triples, but long before Gregg tried his luck on the 750s, Kenny Blake took the flag at Bathurst in 1970 on his H1R, knocking five seconds off the existing class record in the process. Like Molloy in the GP 500 class, the racers down under could see that the two-strokes were the next big thing, plus they were adept at making the things hold together for the duration of the race.

Vive La France

Others in Europe could see potential in the new Kawasaki triples. French racer and engineer Eric Offenstadt was arguably the most innovative developer of the H1R 500 in the early '70s, with his aluminium monocoque-framed special. This was way ahead of its time, as tubular cradle frames, essentially unchanged in their basic design from Victorian bicycles, were the norm. To be fair, Ossa had beaten Eric to it with its monocoque-framed 250 back in '67, but the Spanish machine had conventional

Eric Offenstadt made a monocoque alloy chassis for the triple engine. (Courtesy Eric Offenstadt)

Note the laid-down shocks, cast wheels and disc brakes; all advancd stuff for the early '70s. (Courtesy Eric Offenstadt)

117

THE KAWASAKI TRIPLES BIBLE

Baranne was a sponsor in partnership with Sidemm, the Kawasaki importer in France, and promoted the brand through road racing. (Courtesy Eric Offenstadt)

Christian Ravel, who could, perhaps, have been the first French 500cc GP World Champion, but his career was short.

brakes and an engine that was set bolt upright in its frame.

Eric had learned much of the principles behind the use of a box-section, cast alloy, spine frame from his years racing with Matra, and watching car teams like Lotus. He also fitted drilled disc brakes to his bike, which was still quite rare in '71, despite UK racer Dave Croxford winning a race with a disc brake bike as far back as 1966. The Offenstadt also had modified forks and a wider fairing, which went against received wisdom of the time, but the boxy, aluminium chassis was wide in order to accommodate the gas tank. Eric explained his thinking to the bike press in 2009: "I learned from masters like Colin Chapman at Lotus. The monocoque chassis was the logical solution to the H1R's heavy, tall frame. I instinctively placed the engine further forward, to improve handling. It was obvious disc brakes were better than drums, although many riders didn't believe they would work in the wet at the time. In '71 we added cast wheels, even though there were many who thought they might crack and fail. Some did, but that's progress; you have to push things. Michelin was totally against me using tubeless tyres as well, but the H1R was so much better – it all worked."

The Offenstadt machine had the engine canted forward at a steep angle, with two support tubes running down from the front of the monocoque section to the engine, whilst two alloy plates secured the rear of the motor. It was unique and controversial at the time, but undeniably successful, with podium places in Austria, Belgium and Spain the proof. Eric finished a respectable 6th in the '71 500cc World Championship.

The following year development continued with magnesium alloy cast wheels replacing old-fashioned spokes, and in '73 Eric had a H2R 750 motor cut up, utilising two cylinders from it, then adding his own six speed gearbox. He also began experimenting with alternatives to conventional front forks. Eric posted a 4th place in the Czechoslovakian GP, which turned out to be the last decent GP result for the air-cooled H1R 500 race machine.

Although the 1971 Offenstadt H1R 500 never won a GP, its effect on road racing was far-reaching. Over the next decade, specialists like Terry Shepherd, Nico Bakker, Antonio Cobas, and others refined monocoque alloy frames to show road racers that the days of tubular frames were definitely over.

The racers

Apart from Dave Simmonds, another potential GP winner for Kawasaki was French racer Christian Ravel, who won the French 500cc National Championship in 1970 on an H1R. Ravel's brief racing career on the Kawasaki H1R was cut short, but unlike Offenstadt or Simmonds, Ravel was a rider who simply rode around inherent handling problems – and the H1R had them.

Ravel told the French biking press that competing in a GP race in 1970 on the Kawasaki was no picnic. "It is a tall bike, by which I mean that it carries its weight high in the frame, which makes it hard to handle – harder than the MV. Also, power delivery is not so flexible."

By setting the H1R's engine, which was also fairly wide, so high in the frame, and then adding a hefty fuel load, the H1R was compromised from the word go. Even balls-of-steel riders such as Rusty Bradley, DuHamel, and Ravel struggled to tame it. At the Ulster GP in 1970, Ravel crashed on one of the fast straights, recalling to the press that "the cause of the accident remains a mystery, but we can only assume that the bike landed crossed-up, after hitting a bump. I cannot remember the accident, but I was lucky to sustain only a foot injury in that crash after hitting a tree."

Ravel's luck ran out at Spa in '71. He was battling for 2nd place on his H1RA, racing in close company against Jack Findlay and Eric Offenstadt. Ravel's machine apparently ran out of fuel halfway around a 120mph corner on the Belgian track. It's possible that the engine partially seized, but, either way, he lost control, hit the hay bales then fell back onto the circuit, sustaining multiple injuries. He died later in hospital.

Talking tech; classic racer's view

The H1R was based on the road model H1 500, but had a more potent engine, close ratio gearbox, and some work to its chassis to try and iron out inherent handling problems. Was it a true contender?

Dave Crussell, who has successfully raced restored H1Rs in vintage events across the USA says 'yes.' "The frame, which is based on A1R/A7R tubework, is really very similar to a Norton featherbed lowboy chassis." says Dave, "The most obvious difference between the road based 500 and the H1R's frame are the downtubes, which are set much wider than the road-based 500's tubes."

Other points worth noting on the H1R's frame is how similar the headstock bracing is to a late '60s Rickman design, with a distinct and heavy triangulated section where top rails and downtubes meet at the steering head. The H1R also had a strong bracing bar placed just below the carbs. Early H1R bikes also had their top rails set wider than the road model, which helped accommodate a section of fuel tank hanging between the rails, that lowered the overall mass a touch and offered greater fuel capacity, which the H1R definitely needed.

The H1R had thicker forks than the road model, with firmer internals, again, based closely on the Ceriani design of the '60s. According to Dave Crussell: "Some of the US racers in '71 ordered H1R machines minus forks, wheels and brakes, and fitted Ceriani forks and Fontana disc/drum brakes themselves. It became a kind of

Rusty Bradley's H1R, restored by Dave Crussell. (Courtesy Dave Crussell)

119

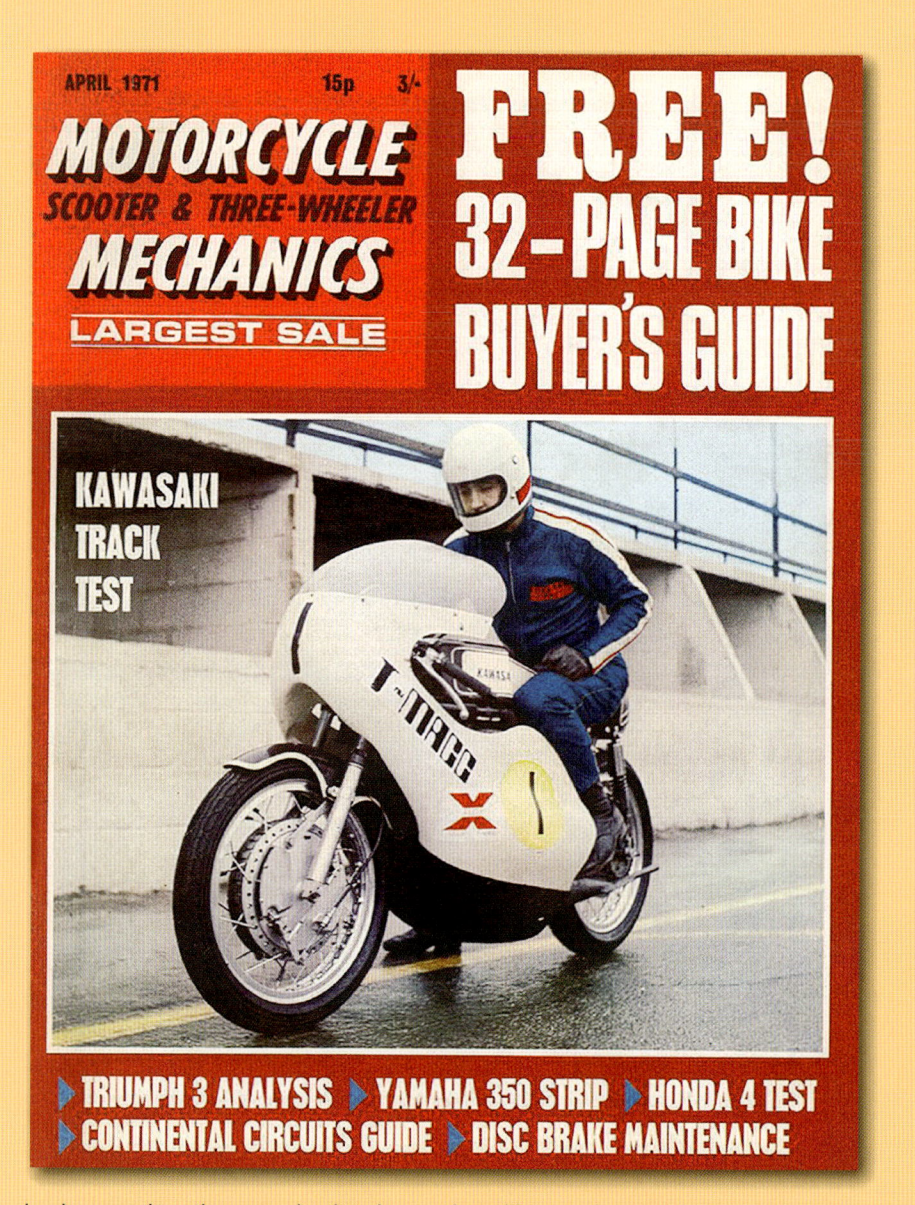

standard upgrade – then you had a decent handling and powerfully braking race machine."

Engine-wise, there was plenty in common with the H1 500 launched in September '68. The H1R motor varied in key areas, of course, and featured cast iron cylinder liners, race-spec pistons and rings, plus enlarged transfer ports. It also ran a battery and three coils, rather than the road model's electronic ignition, and had a stronger bottom end with a beefed-up lube system spraying oil into the roller-bearing crankshaft and toughened con-rods, whilst the carbs sucked in 20:1 premix fuel.

A close ratio, five speed gearbox and dry clutch kept things simple as regards transmission, and the H1R breathed in via rubber-mounted Mikuni 35mm carbs. Many racers fitted 36mm carbs once they'd figured out how to do some porting and exhaust work to squeeze more power from the motor. At its launch in late 1969, Kawasaki officially claimed 75bhp at 9000rpm from the H1R. It doesn't sound much now, but it's debatable whether MVs of the time were making much more than that, so the H1R was a genuine GP contender – in the right hands.

Hammering metal in the cauldron of Daytona

Kawasaki might not have backed a factory road racing team, but it did offer huge amounts of prize money in the USA, which was far and away the company's number one target market between 1965 and 1975.

Canadian racer Yvon DuHamel later recalled how tempted he was to race the Team Hansen H1R in 1971. "I worked out that if I won the number one plate I would net $100,000 – I'd never heard of winning that much money from motorcycle racing."

At the opening of the 1970 season, Kawasaki USA announced a total prize fund of some half a million dollars for winners riding a Kawasaki. By contrast, a European racer like Tommy Robb earned around $500-$1000 for a Grand Prix podium place – just enough to survive.

The H1R was developed by a small team of engineers from Japan, based in the USA throughout 1969, and featured a frame based on the A1R twin. The main problems were weight distribution and soft suspension, which made it hard to handle, plus a reliance on drum brakes rather than trying to use discs. On the upside, the H1R was relatively cheap to buy, and there was a realistic chance of winning a slice of the $500,000 contingency cash, which meant there were lots of riders willing to do Kawasaki's development work in the 1970 season.

In the words of Chip Furlong, who raced an H1R in the USA, 1970-72, the bike – for all its faults – was a potential race-winner: "Very competitive and you didn't have to sell the farm to own one. It was fast and way cheaper than an MV Agusta."

But one thing which bugged early H1R owners was the lack of spares for the fragile engines. "No, there were no spares or 'kits' from Kawasaki in 1970." recalls Chip. " The following year when Kawasaki hired Bob Hansen, things changed slightly. Basically, if Bob Hansen liked you or thought you might be up-and-coming, he would give, or sell you things from time to time. At one point, he had a bunch of stock 500 Mach III heads modified to H1R spec so they could be called in and inspected if they won the race. He gave me a set of these heads."

Like Ginger Molloy in the GP circus in Europe, Chip found that the H1R's ignition wasn't as great as it could have been. "In 1970 I ran the bike stock. In '71 I had the factory CDI unit, which at times had me pushing the bloody thing into the first turn before it would light the plugs. One time at Daytona in '72, I showed Jess Thomas how I checked a black box, by just holding one up and rattling it. None of us knew what we were doing in those days. If I'd had my head on right, I'd have gone back to points. Kevin Cameron ran a Krober set-up, I believe, and he used to put ice over the whole area to keep it cool."

Daytona back then was a super-fast speed bowl, with a short infield section, a real cauldron of speed – and courage – where riders would hit over 160mph on the famous banking. Tuning two-strokes and holding them flat out on the banking was always a knife-edge gamble.

"In '71 I removed 20mm out of the header pipes," says Chip, "and the engine revved higher, which was great. Sadly, it also removed the pins that located the piston rings, and soon a shower of debris rained down on the crank. In that winter of '71-72, I followed Kevin Cameron's advice and elongated the ports, then raised them on each side so the window wouldn't catch the piston rings. I also followed Fast Eddie Moran's advice and moved the engine forward. That was good advice, but Eddie persuaded me to obtain two H1RA frames and said he would make some mods to my frame, based on a section of BSA A65 tube work he admired.

"Eddie did the job and I prepared the bike for the 1972 Daytona meeting. Apparently, this frame modification was a bad idea. First, I thought it was me, but there was an almost constant speed wobble over 130mph. On the first lap of the race, I had to get off the gas on the back straight just to regain control. It ended soon enough with a derailed chain and a 'beginning of the end' feeling in the pit of my stomach. I quit

Ed Moran has a thoughtful cigarette, as Larry Koup waits on the bike at Daytona. (Courtesy Chip Furlong)

professional racing at the next meeting, Road Atlanta."

Chip describes a unique experience of battling with the H1R at Daytona. "We rode into the banking at something like 160mph. The H1R was the first bike I'd ridden where you really needed to pick a line there. On the banking, the suspension compressed and double vision hit you. I always tried to go in very high, so I'd stay away from the wall coming out of the fourth turn of the oval.

"Two things always happened simultaneously: the front wheel seemed to want to come up, and the bike wanted to be sucked into the wall. All this whilst flat out, as the bike wiggled and threatened a full tank-slapper. I'd stick my knee out into the wind and lean the best I could. I was always so relieved to head back into the infield where I could start racing again, instead of playing that silly, scary craps game on the banking."

> **Collector's notes**
> Firstly, most H1Rs will have been extensively modified. The chances of locating one that has been untouched for four decades are remote. Rather than search for 'originality,' collectors should trace the provenance of the machine as closely as possible to establish its value. Key questions to ask are: who raced it, and, more importantly, who modified it.
> The 1970 production numbers of the first H1R (the most potentially valuable) are a moot point. The Kawasaki factory refuses to say, and estimates vary from around 40 to as many as 60 bikes in total. What we do know is that nearly all of them came without any spare parts. Some USA-purchased H1Rs arrived without wheels or brakes, which is why they were raced with Fontana brakes. If podium finishers like Ginger Molloy couldn't get spare parts from Kawasaki, then it also seems likely that some 1970 H1Rs were almost certainly cannibalised as soon as they were uncrated.
> Chip Furlong recalls several teams and riders getting parts made, from early on in the '70 season. Kevin Cameron, who worked as a development engineer for Kawasaki USA's racing team, agrees: "We had frames, swing arms, gas tanks, cylinder heads, made from scratch. We designed our own exhaust pipes – I still have the drawings, in fact – but each rider back then probably had a different set of ideas about pipe shape, length, fittings, rubber mounts – nothing was standardized then.
> "We also sourced different carbs, replacement pistons and rings for the H1R. Parts were ever-changing on the H1Rs, the failure rate was extremely high right from the start, really. It was part of racing – just figuring out how to make it fast, handle better, and keep it going."
> Kawasaki dealer, racer and east coast Service Manager Ed Moran raced the Kawasaki A1R twin, before developing the H1 and H1R racer. Once Ed got an H1R, he immediately made changes to it. "I welded an extra brace across the rear downtubes of the frame's cradle, and I guess it helped handling a bit. But running a rear tyre on the front was the one thing that seemed to really help the bike's stability. I'd seen Mark Brelsford do that on a Harley, and it made the H1R feel like the front wheel was 'driven' somehow.
> "I also fitted a complete set of one-off, 'quarter-turn' fasteners to the gas tank, bodywork, engine cases – just to save time at the track when you had to tear the thing down to fix it."
> Collectors need to ask searching questions to anyone selling an 'original, factory spec H1R.' The harsh truth is that there's probably no such thing ...

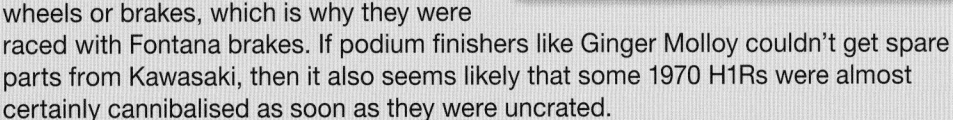

Larry Koup in action at the '70 Daytona meeting. (Courtesy Koup's Motorcycles)

The Kawasaki Triples Bible

H1R 500; official factory specification

Larry at Pocono in '72; by this time he had switched to using disc brakes. (Courtesy Koup's Motorcycles)

Engine
Two-stroke, three cylinder, 498cc, 60x58.8mm bore and stroke. Compression; 7.5:1. Two-ring, lightweight pistons, offset gudgeon pins. 14-roller big end bearings, in copper-plated cage. (This was often changed to silver plating by US H1R racers, as well as silver plating the little ends on the con-rods.) Five transfer ports per cylinder.

Fuel
Pre-mix at 20:1 ratio, 97-octane fuel recommended. Direct oil pump force-feed to main bearings. Ignition; battery, three coils, three sets of points. (Note: many racers replaced points with a Krober ignition.) Sparkplugs; NGK BH10EN grade. Claimed power; 75bhp @9000rpm.

Gearbox
5 speed close ratio, one-down, four-up pattern. Dry clutch. X3 Mikuni VM35S carbs, rubber-mounted. (Many H1Rs were immediately fitted with larger 36mm bore carbs.)

Chassis
Updated A1RA tubular frame with 35mm diameter aluminium Ceriani-type forks, twin rear shocks. Lengthened swing arm. Brakes; 280mm 4LS front drum brake, SLS rear drum. Wheels/tyres; 3.00 section front tyre, 3.50 section rear, 18-inch diameter rims. Dry weight; 135kg, typical race weight with fuel; 145kg.

H1R-A

Faster, but still fragile

For the '71 race season Kawasaki offered privateers the upgraded H1R-A and H1R-AS race bikes, with a claimed 80bhp. The main changes were Kokusan CDI ignition replacing the three sets of points; a redesign of the crankshaft assembly and main bearings; now running 18 rollers, and improved oil flow. Compression had been upped slightly and the bike now made a claimed 80bhp at 9500rpm.

There were many other changes inside the engines throughout the '71 season, as Kevin Cameron recalls: "The reason for working so hard on the engine was simple; we had a long list of failures in the '70 season. Poor lubrication and holed pistons were the big problems. Twelve H1Rs started in the Amateur 100 mile race, six finished, two of which were in the top ten and four in the top fifteen. In the Expert 200 there were ten H1Rs and five finishers."

Not a great finishing rate, although nobody knew how fragile the big H2Rs would prove back then. The '71 season H1R-A was essentially a kitted-up model, with new cylinder linings, carbs, main bearings, exhausts, and electronic ignition. The entire kit cost the aspiring road racer $550; expensive but not financially crippling.

"The ignition wasn't great," recalls Kev Cameron, "and I think it was Cliff Carr who brought over a Krober ignition box. That either worked straight away or rapidly fried its rectifier diodes. The factory items weren't much good. Much of the improvements on the H1R-A can be put down to the work Freddy Mitchell at Boston Cycles did on Rusty Bradley's machine; that would pull 9000rpm against the wind at Daytona in '70 – nobody else had an H1R which could rev close to that."

Rusty Bradley's H1RA; a quick bike for a fast rider. (Courtesy Dave Crussell)

CHAPTER ELEVEN

THE H2R RACERS

Mark Brelsford and Larry Darr collide in spectacular fashion at Daytona in '73. Both riders survived.

"It was war" is how Kevin Cameron, who worked as a technician for various Kawasaki race teams in the early '70s, describes the fearsome battle for supremacy between Suzuki, Yamaha and Kawasaki on the racetracks of the USA. Frames and tyres struggled to cope with 100bhp or more, engines exploded, machines caught fire and, ultimately, riders died, sadly.

For some, it was all just part of racing. Gary Nixon gave me a short interview about his Kawasaki triple racing days, and summed up the experience in a few pithy sentences.

"I didn't give a shit who built the bikes, I just raced 'em. Yeah, they were fast bikes, but hell, the H2Rs were only 30mph faster than a BSA triple, it was no big deal. There was never time to be scared, anyone who was scared of those bikes had no business being out there. The Transatlantic Match Races? Probably fun, but I was so jet-lagged I only woke up when the engines started – can't recall a damn thing about any of them. Did I win any of 'em?"

The H2R built on the success and inherent failings of the H1R/A. As documented in the chapter on the H1R, it proved equally as fragile in the heat of battle, and handled fairly badly. When the H2R was announced for '72, everyone in road racing could see this would be a more serious machine, but the H1R performances at Daytona in '71 must have given people food for thought; Rusty Bradley died in a crash and Cliff Carr managed a 15th place finish. The omens weren't good. But Suzuki had built the TR750, based on the GT750 'water buffalo' engine: the future was two-strokes, like it or not.

The AMA decided to run its '72 National Road Race Championship along broadly similar lines to the F750, the production-based series that BSA/Triumph, Harley and Honda machinery battled in. Everyone could see that Americans liked big road bikes, so it made sense to bump up interest in big capacity road racing. Kawasaki drummed up some pre-race publicity by

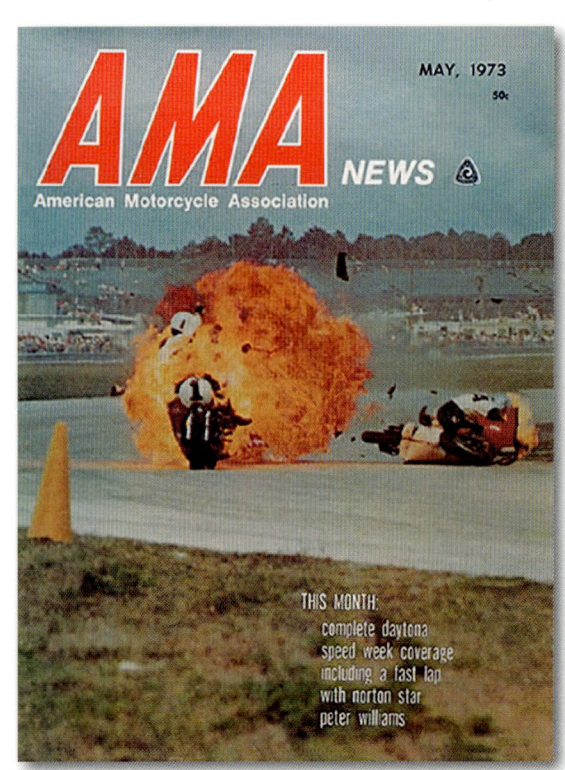

THE H2R RACERS

holding 'secret' H2R tests in late '71 at an American track.

Accelerated development

As with the frantic dash to get the H1R up and running shortly after launching the H1 500, Kawasaki spent a large part of '71 building a new H2R motor to go racing. It had to be based on the road bike engine, as the AMA F750 rules stated that the stock head, cases and cylinder castings had to be retained, but that still left the capacity for a decent amount of potential tuning and fitting of upgraded parts, such as clutch, six-speed gearbox, pistons, carbs, exhausts, etc.

Lessons were learned from the H1R failures in '70, and the 750 race motor had a stronger crank assembly with 14 rollers, larger, polished crank fillets, and welded up, ribbed crankcases. A gearbox made of higher grade alloy cogs, using a new grinding process and fresh shims to make selection more positive, fed power through a 12-plate racing clutch.

Hurley Wilvert ready to rock 'n' roll at Daytona in '74. Note the drilled rear disc. Steve Whitelock had seen early iron discs being drilled by car racer Dan Gurney, and suggested Team Hansen adopt the practice to save weight. (Courtesy Chip Furlong)

127

Kawasaki spent weeks trying different transfer port shapes to improve combustion and scavenging. In an ideal world, it would probably have used a new set of barrels and revised port layout, but was stuck with using the stock H2 four port design, and couldn't make them too wide. Wide ports need bridges to stop the piston rings from pushing into the gaps, then the rings wear rapidly, maybe break, causing a seizure at high rpm. Ouch ...

So if bridged ports weren't allowed, what did that leave? The only real answer was to get the H2R motor pumping faster, to shove more gas and air through the engine. To combat the chances of catastrophic seizures at high revs, compression was lowered to 6.6:1, which also made the bike slightly less of a pig to push-start. As long as the engine could be cooled sufficiently, the crankshaft strengthened and the ignition timing set spot-on, everything would be fine – in theory.

Like the H1R, the H2R motor had rubber-mounted, 35mm carbs (Mikuni designed these originally for snowmobile use) to try and prevent frothing. The CDI electronic ignition was modified, retarded substantially from stock H2 settings. The ignition failures the H2R suffered were mainly vibration-related, according to Kevin Cameron, but interestingly, when Stan Shenton was asked by Kawasaki UK to race the '74 H2R, he added parts from a Triumph Trident generator to make the bike easier to bump-start. "You had to run alongside at 30mph to get the thing to start with its stock ignition," Shenton told *Classic Racer* in the late '80s.

An air-cooled, two-stroke is something of a hand grenade in engineering terms. Any breathing or mixture difficulties tend to fry the pistons, usually near the exhaust ports first, where temperatures can be fiendishly hot, and uneven on something like a triple. So one cylinder may suffer 'hot spots' whilst the other two are fine, for example. The centre pot is always the favourite for overheating. Part of Kawasaki's solution to managing H2R gas flow was to alter the shape of the exhaust pipes from those used on the H1R, to ones with a less pronounced bulge in the mid-section. The theory was the pipes would help make the motor less peaky, more torquey and help clear the combustion chamber of spent gases at just the right fraction of a second, allowing a fresh charge in there. Did they work? Well, most H2R race teams in '72 would throw these pipes in the bin and make their own from scratch.

As racers and pit mechanics recall from the era: "Everyone had a different view on H2R exhausts; racing two-strokes was a lottery, especially the bigger ones. What worked at one track, didn't seem to match up the next."

The H2R engine was bench and dyno tested, with a nice round 100bhp quoted as official output by Kawasaki. It was, perhaps, nearer 90bhp, but it's academic since most of the early H2Rs blew themselves up within a few hundred racing miles. It was unfortunate that workshop and brief '71 track tests failed to show up key problems which would cause Team Hansen and others long nights of headaches. Chief amongst these were con-rod and big-end failure, and

Eric Offenstadt at Daytona in '73 on a factory, H2R-engined race machine.

THE H2R RACERS

One of Dave Crussell's triples collection, an early H2R featuring the slimmer, more rounded fairing and massive front discs. (Courtesy Dave Crussell)

the gearbox selector mechanism proved temperamental, too.

"They silver-plated the big-end cages, but they were still weak, as were the con-rods." commented Kevin Cameron in 2010, "The forged pistons Kawasaki used in the H2R weren't good either. It took them far too long to realise that they couldn't trust their suppliers 100 per cent. Even as late as '74 I recall seeing a French team fire up a new H2R and it seized on the stand: there was a mad scramble to grab pistons and barrels from the preceding year."

Paul Smart recalls how fragile the '72 HR2s were. "Usually a big-end or the small-ends would break up, the bits would then lock up the engine. But we didn't even have decent two-stroke oil; we used Castrol R."

Classic racer Dave Crussell, who has won plenty of races on his H2R ,says he uses Yamaha RD400 con-rods to get around that particular problem. Crussell also worked on the handling of the H2R for classic racing in the modern era, by moving the H2R engine forward in the frame, and using fairly soft rear shocks to improve handling.

"The original H2Rs ran with hard, near rigid, shocks," relates Crussell, "and all that seemed to do was transmit force into the frame when it hit the bumps, then the bike wiggled. Modern suspension, with softer settings, works well. Really, the H2R frame isn't that bad – it's based on a Norton featherbed, after all."

'72: frames, what frames?

Kawasaki had problems with the chassis – there wasn't one. You can only imagine the faces of Team Hansen when they unpacked the crates from Japan just weeks before Daytona '72. The new engine wasn't that great either, but at least it arrived – in the nick of time.

So, at Daytona, Team Hansen was forced to use a H1RA chassis, with H2 750 road forks, wheels, and extremely heavy cast iron disc brakes based on Honda units. They simply slotted the new H2R motor in once it arrived and headed out to practice. As Kevin Cameron relates, the bikes were worryingly slow, struggling to break 150mph – slower than the H1R.

Speed proved academic, however, as the 200-mile race saw Team Hansen's

Nixon, Smart and Du Hamel all retire with tyre and drivechain problems, it was much the same shredded rubber story for the big Suzuki triples. Tyre companies were totally unprepared for these new, high powered two-strokes. The state-of-the-art technology then was a tyre shaped like a Toblerone chocolate triangle – the theory was that the flat sides would offer more grip when leaned over.

"You would go out in practice to set some fast times," recalls Paul Smart, "the bike would get this strange vibration then, bang – the tyres would break up. It was terrifying."

As the big machines dropped out with utterly ruined tyres at Daytona '72, Don Emde took the win on a Yamaha TZ350. It was a race which made Dunlop and Goodyear go away and invent the racing slick in '73; what the tyre companies had just didn't work anymore.

Things could only improve for Team Hansen and they did, rapidly. Bob Hansen and Randy Hall were nothing if not quick learners and arch wheeler-dealers in the procurement of parts and expertise. The Kawasaki base at Santa Ana, just south of LA, was a hive of activity as riders, mechanics, frame and suspension specialists frantically worked out solutions to the inherent problems of making the H2R a race winner. At Daytona, Smart and Nixon ran without front fenders to try and cool the motor, but the fairing was re-designed to try and funnel more air in, as fenders had to be fitted, under the rules. You can spot the bigger fairing by its distinctive 'lip' set under the exhaust header pipes. It also has a wider set of glass fibre panels all round, designed to suck in and expel air as rapidly as possible.

Although Dunlop and Goodyear took another year to figure out slicks, in the meantime, using wider rim cast magnesium wheels allowed fatter, rounder profile tyres, and new compounds – especially on the crucial sidewall areas – could be tried out. There were still tyre problems, but the rubber got better.

Frank Camillieri and Colin Seeley arguably proved the best frame builders for the H2R, but not before Randy Hall had a frame made from heavy gauge steel tubes, which one rider (who shall remain nameless) wryly described as "like sections of sewer pipe."

"The bike must have weighed about 40lb more, it still didn't handle." adds the racer, who rated Camillieri's frames as the best he had ever tried. Bracing bars were welded on, extra gusseting used, but the H2R still shimmied like a pig on roller skates once you tried cornering at high speed.

According to legend, the Colin Seeley-framed bike used by Paul Smart to win at Ontario in '72 solved the problem. But is this entirely true?

The victory was – like many a race win – a lucky one, since Cliff Carr was leading the second leg of the race, on the Camillieri-framed Arlington Sports H2R, until it blew its crankshaft. But Smart's famous win definitely caused a problem between him and Team Hansen. Smart was something of a junior rider in the set-up, and getting a frame made showed a stubborn level of independence and determination to do things his own – and not the team – way.

Smart told *Motorcycle Mechanics* in late '72 that he hoped to be riding the H2R in '73, again, using Hurley Wilvert as his crew man, and furthermore added that the "H2R's handling is now sorted out."

Instead, he was fired and went to Suzuki for the '73 season. Today, Paul Smart looks back on that '72 season. "Bob Hansen was as tight as a duck's bum," recalls Paul, "and he was delighted that I paid for the Seeley frame out of my own pocket. I had Colin knock up the frame in three weeks flat, then dropped the engine in. Easy.

"It was an improvement, but, with hindsight, the problem wasn't so much the frame as the suspension. We did some good work with Kat Kayaba that season, and also looked into using motocross shocks, because there was an MX team near the Kawasaki shop in Santa Ana. Thing is, nobody really knew what they were doing back then – it was all partly guesswork."

The root cause of the H2R's weaving and wriggling was almost certainly a lack of shock and fork damper travel, plus a fluent, responsive ride quality – things taken for granted today on multi-adjustable, gas-damped suspension systems. You hit a bump on the H2R, Suzuki TR750, or the early Yamaha TZ700 and the entire bike moved, the suspension fed the energy almost directly to the frame.

"You were just paid to ride the bikes," adds Paul Smart, "and do nothing much else. You could adjust the preload on the shocks and that was it. But it was still the era when a semi-factory outfit could try out different things.

"That's what frustrated me, I could see Yamaha joining F750 in '73 maybe, so Kawasaki's chance to score big wins was that moment, the '72 season. It took such a long time for Kawasaki Japan to do things itself, and when an improvement was figured out the answer was generally 'we will try that next year, thank you.' I just thought I'd get on with it, make the bike better and win some races."

Paul recalls Kawasaki did send over technicians to study the H2R, and that the Japanese rider, Wada, was "an incredibly brave racer, I don't know how he made that bike go so fast at Daytona."

At the end of '72, Paul moved on to Suzuki, where again he had to work with a certain level of cost control. "I think Gary Nixon used the Seeley frame after I did – even though I owned it. I never got it back. But that was racing then, Suzuki was just the same; myself, Barry Sheene, and Ron Williams at Maxton basically did the development work for them. Whichever factory you rode for back then, they all expected race wins on the cheap and they all politely picked your brains for the best ideas."

Incidentally, Paul Smart and Hurley Wilvert were also paid by Kawasaki to test the prototype Kawasaki 900 Z1 in '72, which led to some road trip-style hi-jinks. "We did thousands of miles across America. We rode two-up and even three-up sometimes when I put my wife, Maggie, on the fuel tank. We took the Z1 around Talladega for high speed testing, and did over 100 miles in under an hour, it would've been a world record if we'd bothered to have it officially recorded. We also entered a little motorcycle club race meeting one weekend, putting our name on the form as 'Team Honda,' and we won! Christ, we got a bollocking for that …"

'73: making progress

The H2R won three races out of seven AMA Grand Nationals in '72, which, from Kawasaki's point of view, was a success. Team Hansen's 'quick fill' refuelling method had cut the time of the extra fuel stops that the H2R needed, and the team also added useful chassis parts such as Morris cast alloy wheels, lighter magnesium carbs, and, after an experiment with drilled iron discs, tungsten-coated alloy brakes from Kawasaki Japan.

Rival Suzuki had problems, too: disqualified in one race, plus engines seized and tyres shredded with much the same frequency as the H2Rs. As Yamaha still didn't have the TZ700 ready for '73, and AMA F750 rules would have made it illegal to use in any case, since it wasn't based on a production machine, Kawasaki decided to take full control of the US road race team for '73, and upped the budget dramatically: this was Kawasaki's shot at taking the AMA title.

A two-tier supported squad of Du Hamel and Baumann, with Nixon, Carr and Wilvert in the B team (Smart's faux pas was Hurley's opportunity there) was put together. Erv Kanemoto was brought in as tuner/bike builder, a brilliant move as he had an uncanny ability to get the best from a big two-stroke. This 'ear' for two-strokes would be put to the test early in '73 at Daytona.

The 200 event started well for the H2Rs. Japanese rider Wada was quickest in the speed trap during practice, and Du Hamel and Baumann battled for the lead early in the race. Then they crashed out and Nixon's and Wada's bikes both seized. The likely culprit was the main bearings, according to technician Cameron, who kept a log of

Art Baumann and Hurley Wilvert raced at Daytona in '73 and '74 aboard H2Rs. Wilvert was more successful, bagging a 3rd place in the '74 200-mile event. (Courtesy Chip Furlong)

failures during his seasons with Kawasaki race bikes. "Kawasaki used larger-than-normal big-end rollers, probably based on the idea that sub-surface shear stress decreases as surface radius of curvature increases. But it's the combined mass of the big-end roller set, plus cage, that determines life in racing. Because the rod swings from side-to-side, the speed of the big-end bearing varies by plus or minus 25 per cent, twice per revolution, and if the big-end bearing is quite heavy, the rollers can't follow the speed change. They then slip, plough oil off the surfaces, and begin to suffer surface damage. An H2R crank with 400 miles was about it – after that, failure could come quickly."

French rider Eric Offenstadt made another attempt at the Daytona 200 in '73, after his H2-powered race machine seized

THE H2R RACERS

its gearbox in the '72 event. That motor was a ported H2 road bike engine, fitted in an alloy monocoque chassis.

"It was pulling 270kph (168mph), then the gears locked up whilst I was in 3rd place," recalls Eric, "so I came back on a factory H2R machine with the backing of Sidemm in '73. This time, I made my own six-speed gearbox just to be on the safe side. But that bike could make only 222kph (138mph). Not fast enough!"

Pistons were another weak area for the H2R, and it took months for Kawasaki to get more durable parts manufactured. But as '73 wore on, the Kawasaki began to hold together and win, taking victories at Laguna, Ontario, Loudon, Pocono and Charlotte. Du Hamel also had the satisfaction of winning at Mosport in Canada.

Suzuki took the first FIM F750 title, however, as Kawasaki concentrated on the US, not Europe. Venturing out of the USA with the H2R wasn't a great success in '73. Although the Transatlantic races, Imola 200 and Silverstone's F750 meeting were all attended, Team Hansen scored only one win, in the Transatlantic Match Races, Du Hamel surprising the British team with his instant speed and take-no-prisoners riding style. A typical gutsy performance was at Silverstone's inaugural F750 round, where the frame cracked on Du Hamel's bike, although he still finished in 2nd place in the opening race, then blew his engine in race two, struggling with a dodgy gearbox. Rather like the road-going H2, the H2R had beautifully made cogs, it was the shift mechanism that seemed to give problems and lock the bike into one gear, or provide false neutrals.

Tellingly, the AMA season was dominated by the Nixon/Kanemoto combination. That bike, running wire wheels and welded wider wheel rims, won at Loudon, Pocono and Laguna Seca. It was Nixon's best season in racing for about five years, and testament to Kanemoto's skill in helping the H2R withstand the heat of battle. Reportedly, Nixon paid Kanemoto half his prize money winnings, he was so glad to make a racing comeback.

Rumours persist that, during '73, some H2Rs had barrels on them with wider ports, featuring bridges, which contravened AMA rules – but there's no proof this happened.

'74: the lost year

After the success of '73, everyone expected Kawasaki to take the fight to Yamaha, which had joined in the F750 series with the TZ750. Instead, Kawasaki drastically scaled back its US road race programme and spent money on building a global distributor network and starting a fledgling UK race operation. Officially, Kawasaki said that because US motorcycle sales fell at the back end of '73, it had to make cutbacks. Realistically, it had little chance of beating the water-cooled Yamaha and Suzuki bikes in '74 – and knew it.

Du Hamel was the only Kawasaki rider for the season, with a pay rise and Randy Hall heading up his team in the pit lane. Kawasaki specified new pistons for the '74 season, but, as the first H2R to use them seized, teams stuck with the '73 versions. Wilvert joined Du Hamel and Baumann at Daytona, and Wilvert's machine, prepped by George Vukmanovich, posted a third place in the 200-mile race. Vukmanovich went on to work for Suzuki and Cagiva GP teams: he knew two-strokes.

Agostini won on the TZ750 at Daytona with Kenny Roberts in second, also on a

Another machine from the Crussell collection. Note the unusual exhaust pipe routing, an interesting dodge to increase ground clearance. (Courtesy Dave Crussell)

Following page: Just $6 to spectate on race day; a bargain. Du Hamel posted a respectable 2nd place at this meeting, the best result of the year.

133

Kawasaki SuperBike International
Laguna Seca Monterey

Don't Miss
The Race of Races
July 26, 27, 28, 1974

Kawasaki SuperBike International

Regular Prices
- Practice & Qualifying ...... Fri. $2
- General Admission .... Sat. $4
- Race Day General Admission... $7
- Paddock................. $2
- Grandstand.............. $2
- TOTAL $17

Available at all Ticketron Outlets
SPECIAL "WEEKENDER" TICKETS ARE GOOD FOR ALL THREE DAYS OF GENERAL ADMISSION, PADDOCK AND GRANDSTAND.

ALL FOR $12.00

OR RACE DAY TICKETS
$6.00 IN ADVANCE

Vacationers!
Camping, hotel, and tourist information in and around the beautiful Monterey Peninsula is available from the Monterey Chamber of Commerce
Call 408-375-2252 or Write: Monterey Chamber of Commerce Box 1770 Monterey, CA 93940

Race Day General Admission — $6.00 in advance, $7.00 at the track

I enclose $_____ (Money Order or Certified Check) for the following:

_____ Super Tickets at $12.00

_____ Race Day General Admissions at $6.00

Name _____

Address _____ Zip Code _____

MAIL TO: Trippe Cox Associates Inc.,
PO BOX 2078,
Monterey, Calif 93940 (408) 373-1811

THE H2R RACERS

TZ. Wilvert's third was poor consolation, somehow, it was obvious the new Yamaha was going to be the bike to beat in '74 – it was fast and reasonably reliable. That reality of having another big two-stroke rival didn't help team morale. Vukmanovich told the US motorcycle press that "Randy Hall doesn't even consider Hurley part of the team, not even after a 3rd place result. It's a constant hassle getting parts."

Baumann's mechanic, Jeff Shetler, pulled no punches later in the season either. "Look at our horrible bikes, we have to use old stuff from last year. It's embarrassing." he told the press.

Kawasaki had brought back Bob Hansen on a freelance basis after Daytona, and off they went to the Transatlantic Match Races in the UK. The H2R could now use the bridge-ported cylinders, after a convenient rule change. New FIM rules also demanded only 25 machines be produced, which gave Kawasaki the chance to make a brand new H2R – a pure race machine that had nothing to do with the antiquated H2 engine or chassis. Remember, the H2R frame was essentially the same tubework Kawasaki wrapped around its A1/A7 twins in the mid '60s, and that was based on a 1950 Norton featherbed frame.

Engine-wise, things were more promising. Kawasaki did have an experimental square four engine, which could have been a real contender in F750 racing. Instead, it chose to liquid cool the old H2 motor – and didn't get around to doing that until '75.

It was, with hindsight, a great opportunity missed, but few people knew in '73 that motorcycle road racing was going to become a truly global, professional sport. There was also the argument that it would ultimately be the 500 GP class, not the new F750 lunacy, that would remain the premier class in motorcycle sport for decades to come. History would show Kawasaki's reluctance was justified, but, at the time, it looked like a lost chance for glory. Kawasaki and Du Hamel had a tough season in '74, as his bike seized twice during the Transatlantic races, he crashed out trying to beat the Yamahas at Talladega, and an extra fuel stop at Paul Ricard in France cost him an F750 victory.

Du Hamel later told the press he "Felt like a hobo in battered leathers," and ended up having a punch-up with a track official in France. Tighter budgets, more sleep-sapping long-haul travel, and an outdated bike were factors that even a racing matador like Du Hamel found difficult to deal with.

Kawasaki came up with a new chassis during the '74 season, the H2R gaining a fashionable box-section swing arm. The shocks were angled down slightly, too, rather than set bolt upright, increasing their travel.

'73 was the comeback year for Gary Nixon on the Kanemoto-prepped H2R. Note the copywriter's use of 'Ken' Roberts, better known to actual bike race fans as Kenny Roberts, of course.

Back on top. Again.

The last AMA National that Gary Nixon won was at Loudon. Three years ago. This year, again at Loudon, the '67 and '68 Grand National Champion regained his winning ways. Grabbing the lead on lap one, Gary held it for 75 miles and the victory. Followed home by Yamaha-mounted Ken Roberts and Triumph's Gary Scott. The number one and two ranked riders on this year's AMA Grand National circuit. Plus this victory moved Gary Nixon up to a strong third in his quest for a third national title.

The spark plugs firing Gary's Kawasaki, Ken's Yamaha and Gary Scott's Triumph were Champions. The brand that's right for every engine.

CHAMPION SPARK PLUGS
Toledo, Ohio 43661

Better plugs for everyone.

135

THE KAWASAKI TRIPLES BIBLE

Kawasaki provided relatively few H2Rs in '74. The UK team effort of Ditchburn and Grant received two, and in Australia the Murray Sayle and Ron Toombs team raced them, with greater reliability than the US H2Rs ever achieved. Gregg Hansford got one of the updated H2R machines in '74, and immediately began to make an impression.

In the '75 season the Aussie H2R racers, tuned by Neville Doyle, managed to win 29 races from 31 starts on their air-cooled H2Rs, but this was overlooked when everyone got excited about the new, water-cooled H2R bikes. That astonishing reliability (maintained in the '76, season by the way) proved the H2R really could have been a race winner, maybe even as dominant as the MV Agusta four in the late '60s, if it had been prepared and truly developed.

The great tragedy of the H2R was the lack of focus from the word go. Kawasaki already knew that the air-cooled two-strokes would suffer horribly in the great speed bowls of America; the H1 road bike and H1R race bike proved it. Kawasaki developed an engine that was powerful enough, but never kept a close eye on race component suppliers to make sure that races weren't lost for the sake of a bearing, or a badly annealed con-rod. Neither would it listen and learn from the riders, technicians, tuners and framebuilders who struggled to make the 180mph motorcycles stay together on the track.

In this respect, Kawasaki was no different to all the other motorcycle manufacturers of the era. A casual glance at motorcycle racing history shows that, whilst riders like Hailwood or Agostini could win on almost anything, it took a Degner, McCandless, Carcano or Cobas to plant the seed of technological progress.

This '73 H2R, owned by a UK collector, was on show at Race Retro in 2007, and is reputedly the Gary Nixon factory Kawasaki. Note the box section swing arm with three positions for the shock mounting.

THE **H2R** RACERS

Collector's notes

The H2R was never produced as a 'kitted' race machine like the H1R. Numbers from the Kawasaki factory are, of course, impossible to obtain, but a total production of about 150 engines, and perhaps 100 frames/chassis, between '71 and '74 seems likely. There were very few H2Rs produced for '72 and engines arrived first: it took Kawasaki a while to get around to making complete bikes.

As the H1Rs were sometimes known to arrive without forks, brakes or wheels, we have to assume the same thing happened with the H2R. Supply increased for '73, Kawasaki's big push meant it probably made a few more, but wasn't actively selling these bikes; all it had to do was keep the team going.

For '74, just 25 bikes had to be made to meet F750 eligibility, and we know Kawasaki lost interest. A handful of machines went to the UK, France and Australia. Three bikes raced at Daytona, and the US race operation centred around Du Hamel. Given Du Hamel's crash and engine destruction rate, we can figure that he went through five or six engines that season, but how many times did they simply bend the frame straight again and send him back out?

One thing every collector should note about any '70s race machine is that parts were altered, replaced or damaged often within hours of the bike arriving from the factory. Paul Smart recalls loaning parts at various race meetings, things like ignition covers, cables, brake calipers, etc, and never getting them back. Kevin Cameron says every H2R rider in the '72 and '73 Daytona meetings had their own exhaust pipes made individually. Eric Offenstadt raced a 500 Kawasaki at the French GP which used two out of three H2 cylinders, plus a homemade, 6 speed gearbox This was typical of the period.

A few H2R engines, built by Kanemoto, appear to have been used in flat track races in '75. It was a handy way to use up remaining engine H2R stocks once the water pumper appeared, and the H2R flat-tracker's success inspired Yamaha to do the same thing with the TZ750. There are replicas of these flat track bikes around using tweaked H2 road bike motors.

Visit Veloce on the web – www.veloce.co.uk / www.velocebooks.com
Details of all books in print • Special offers • New book news • Gift vouchers • Forum

CHAPTER TWELVE

LE COUPE SPORTIF

The Coupe Kawasaki race series went a long way toward building the Kawasaki brand in France, and, in some ways, rekindled a love affair with motorcycling itself across France, after a decade of decline.

Coupe Kawasaki was started in 1971 by Sidemm, the French importer of the Kawasaki brand, run by the dynamic Xavier Maugendre. He founded Sidemm in 1967, importing the W1 and W2 series four-strokes and A1/A7 Samurai/Avengers as the first batch of machines, which he promoted by simply loading the motorcycles into a van and taking them to prospective dealers.

Maugendre couldn't spend a fortune on dealer reps, or trade and consumer advertising; he didn't have that budget. But Maugendre saw a one-make road race series as a quick way of publicising the smaller Kawasaki 350 A7 twins, and later the S2 350 and KH400 triples. It worked spectacularly well, as the Coupe Kawasaki series was immediately successful in France, and many young riders, such as Patrick Pons, made a name for themselves in Coupe Kawasaki before going onto greater things.

Pons, a fairly handy downhill skier at the age of just 16, planned to go car racing when he was 18, having suffered a bad knee injury whilst ski-racing. One day, he saw a new H1 500 in a motorcycle shop and was lovestruck. Pons borrowed money from his family to buy a brand new 500 H1 at the age of 17, after just one year's motorcycling experience and only recently passing his test to allow him to ride bigger machinery on the road.

Pons then entered the road-based H1 in a ten-hour endurance race at Montlhéry in 1971, but crashed spectacularly on his first session, totally wrecking the bike. Undeterred, he raced the 500 again and, in '72, entered the Coupe Kawasaki series on a 350, seeing it as a good way to make a start as a road racer.

Coupe Kawasaki, sponsored by leading magazine *Moto Revue*, proved a success with the biking public in France. It was one of the first one-make road racing series in Europe, offering relatively cheap competition for amateur club level racers, often backed by local dealerships.

Although clubman level racers posted some impressive performances – an unknown by the name of Jacques Gonthier won the very first Coupe Kawasaki race – the series soon attracted road racers like Eric Saul, Patrick Pons, and Christian Sarron, who very much saw Coupe Kawasaki as a stepping-stone to greater racing glory.

The Kawasaki Triples Bible

Start of the first Coupe Kawasaki race at Montlhéry in 1971. (Courtesy Yves Evrard)

Claude Gorry goes bouncing down the track at Reims, minus his helmet, but unhurt. (Courtesy of Yves Evrard, Les Amis de la Coupe Kawasaki)

The first Coupe Kawasaki Championship in 1971 ran over eight rounds, with circuits like Paul Ricard, Montlhéry, Dijon, and Castelet on the calendar. The series started on May 1, 1971 with an opening qualifying round at Bourg en Bresse.

The formula was simple: production-spec Kawasaki A7 350 models, with few modifications and a qualifying race to whittle down the first 45 entrants to 29 for the points-scoring final. This was fairly common practice in production races in France, the UK, and Italy in the seventies, when many riders actually turned up at the track on road bikes, went through scrutineering, and just 'had a go.' Health and Safety wasn't really invented back then …

In terms of publicity, Coupe Kawasaki was an excellent idea. Having Gilles Mallet, a racer/journalist with *Moto Revue* (Mallet finished 3rd in the '71 Coupe Kawasaki A7 Championship) as an entrant guaranteed coverage. Holding the races as a support class for bigger events also helped Coupe Kawasaki catch on with the French public. It was fearsomely close racing, with old fashioned push-starts and plenty of crashes – multiple bike pile-ups were not unknown.

The first year saw the battle for the title go down to the wire, with Alain Meyer taking the '71 Championship. The *Moto Revue* journalist, Mallet, finished 3rd in the rankings. Everyone was looking forward to the next season, as the first batches of the new S2 350 triple had arrived at Sidemm's Paris HQ that autumn.

For 1972, the Avenger twin was replaced with new S2 350 triple and some 90-odd riders, many supported by Kawasaki dealers, committed to the series. Three heat races were needed to pare them to 45 riders eligible to compete in the remaining seven races.

LE COUPÉ SPORTIF

Support from Moto Revue *was crucial to Coupe Kawasaki's immediate success. (Courtesy Yves Evrard)*

Displaying an ability to learn rapidly, Patrick Pons won the '72 title in his debut season, whilst also competing in the national 250cc road racing class. It was a close run thing, however, as Pons had crashed out of contention in some of the early races, so had to fight back to win at the final round held at the Le Mans Bugatti circuit, where five or six riders all battled for victory.

Pons later said "In '72, I gave myself just two years to succeed in motorcycle racing; for me, it was win or crash every time in Coupe Kawasaki."

Patrick Pons went on to campaign in various GP classes, and was F750 Champion in '79: tragically, he was killed in the British GP of 1980. Pons' success was an inspiration to any Coupe Kawasaki competitor, as he proved that anyone could make it through to the big time.

Another rider in the '72 Championship alongside Pons was Alain Berthet, who told the French biking press in later years how he got into the race series. "I bought an Avenger A7 new in 1970, but riding around Paris I was constantly pulled over by the police, who behaved like complete bastards towards us. So, fed up with road riding, I bought a 350 triple and went racing in 1972. My only claim to fame was beating Pons in that final race at Bugatti. He fell off twice and so finished well down the order. I was in eighth place – a kind of victory."

In '73 there were 125 entries for Coupe Kawasaki, such was its popularity – everyone could see that battling your way to victory in this series gained attention from road racing teams. Dunlop and Motul got involved in sponsorship deals for the series, too. The winner in '73 was Jean Claude Meilland, and, as well as the trophy and a cheque, he received a new H2 750 from Sidemm. Runners-up in 2nd and 3rd places got Kawasaki KE 125 trail bikes.

The series worked brilliantly in terms of publicity, and sold the 350 S2 to young, speed-crazy riders like Christian Estrosi, who bought one in 1972, aged just 17. He wanted to race it in the Coupe Kawasaki series but, as the age limit was 18, Estrosi had to enter the 250 class on an S1. He finished 5th at Circuit Paul Ricard, then went racing in '73 on an H2R, eventually becoming a Grand Prix rider and Deputy Mayor of Nice.

Other riders who went on to find racing fame after a stint in Coupe Kawasaki included Marc Fontan, Christian Sarron, and Eric Saul. The series was more than just a proving ground for young talent; it was part of a renaissance of interest in motorcycling across France, which had declined in popularity in the '60s as cars replaced motorbikes as everyday transport. Events like the Bol d'Or endurance were huge in terms of prestige, visitor attendance, and works team involvement by the end of the '70s. Riders like Godier, Chemarin and others became international stars as a result of their success in the world of endurance. Heady days ...

1974 saw the launch of the 400 S3, and it was again a hard-fought battle for 45 riders, with Bernard Sailler emerging as champion. The following year was the high point of the series, with some 275 entrants putting their names down for a tilt at the title.

To select a more manageable entry list, a special Coupe Kawasaki weekend was held at Magny Cours, where riders set their fastest times. 135 riders were picked to go forward to a knockout event in which just 45 would compete in the full season's racing. AGV Helmets became a sponsor,

THE KAWASAKI TRIPLES BIBLE

Patrick Pons was one of the stars who came through the ranks of the Coupe Kawasaki series.

Yves Evrard and his sons about to take to the track at Chimay, at one of the Coupe Kawasaki celebratory weekends. (Courtesy Yves Evrard)

and two special invitation races against European riders at Spa and the Bol d'Or were added to the schedule. The top rider from each meeting won an AGV helmet, and made 'Samurai of the meeting' for their exceptional riding, or spectacular crashing. Eric Saul won the overall championship in '75 and, like many other Coupe Kawasaki graduates, went on to GP racing.

There were yet more entrants in '76 and '77, with over 300 attending the special 'shoot-out' days to try and make the final 45 riders list. By this time, two classes of KH400 were allowed; one modified with fairings, upgraded brake systems, and some engine tuning allowed, the other class, much closer to the original spirit of production racing, simply allowed rear sets, pipe bending for ground clearance, and removal of indicators and lights.

1978 was the final year for the purely triples-only Coupe Kawasaki as, for the '79 season, Sidemm decided to promote the Z650 four by making it the headline machine. It wasn't as successful, mainly because the Z650 was singularly unsuited to road racing. After having a go with the four-stroke Scorpion 250s, the Coupe series folded in the early '80s, but was then revived with the K1RS water-cooled two-stroke twin. Kawasaki France run a Coupe series today, utilising the ER6/Versys 650cc twin.

After running Sidemm for some 15 years, Xavier Maugendre sold out to C Itoh & Co (the Kawasaki shipping agent formerly based in London) in 1982, and soon afterward Kawasaki France was set up.

Le Coupé Sportif

An association called Les Amis de la Coupe Kawasaki (LADLC) was formed in France in the '90s to celebrate the spirit of the series, and many ex-competitors ride some of the original bikes at Chimay and other circuits across France. LADLC Chairman Yves Evrard can be seen below with his four sons at Chimay in 2006. Kawasaki KR1S 250cc machines, as well as 350 twins, and 400 triples can all attend.

This Coupe Kawasaki machine was in action at Spa Bikers Classics in 2009. A special round at Spa was held during the '70s series so that the best riders could showcase their skills at an international meeting.

Visit Veloce on the web – www.veloce.co.uk / www.velocebooks.com
Details of all books in print • Special offers • New book news • Gift vouchers • Forum

143

CHAPTER THIRTEEN

THE UK KH400 RACE SERIES

"Kawasaki UK thought a KH400 race series would generate some spares business"
Tony Jakeman

Riders were generally on a tight budget, so improvising transport by ripping the seats out of a Triumph Dolomite was one solution.

Kawasaki UK had seen the success of the French Coupe Kawasaki series and knew it would be a good way of shifting the hard-to-sell KH400 model for the 1978-79 seasons.

"We had dealers selling KH400 models for just £30 more than a KH250 at the time." recalls Tony Jakeman, who organised the series for Kawasaki UK. "It wasn't a popular model and discounting on the KH400 was rife. We knew in late '77 that production in Japan was probably going to cease on the 400 triple in '78, so we thought a one-make series would be a good way to publicise the bike, and sell off remaining stocks to a two-stroke triples fan base."

But the KH400 wasn't a natural choice for club racing in the UK back then. "The KH400 was outclassed by the RD250/400

THE UK KH400 RACE SERIES

bikes which dominated club racing in the UK at that time," recalls Tony, "I have to admit that Kawasaki UK also thought a KH400 race series would generate some more spares business for us as well. We did well with the KH250 on that front as it was very popular with learner riders and they crashed frequently. As the 400 used many common parts, we thought a race series was a winner in that respect, too."

The Kawasaki 400 race series format was essentially production based. Modifications were limited to fitting clip-on-type 'bars, cutting down the seat, tucking in the exhausts to increase ground clearance, and removing the stands and fitting rear set footrests. No engine tuning was allowed, except one cylinder bore over stock. Blueprinting the

Tony Jakeman from Kawasaki UK also competed in the series, and was featured on the cover of this club meeting programme at Cadwell Park in June '79.

After a crash Tony's KH400 was suitably battle-scarred, requiring a new seat, tailpiece, and other bits and pieces.

145

The Kawasaki Triples Bible

The KH400 was one of the first machines to have a one make race series started around it, inspiring other manufacturers to follow suit in the UK during the '80s and '90s. This is Lee Doxey's beautifully restored machine. (Courtesy Lee Doxey)

The UK KH400 Race Series

Daytona Kawasaki rider Neil Williams on the well turned out, dealer-sponsored machine. Note the Z1000 proddie racer in the background to the left.

The essential rider briefing; note the deluxe race control caravan.

engine was permitted. No race compound tyres, just road legal rubber, and no chassis tweaks beyond fitting a steering damper and replacing the soft rear shock absorbers.

The series began with fourteen rounds spread over a mix of circuits, from the GP class Silverstone to the decidedly outdated Wellesbourne. Some £2000 in total prize money was on offer, with cash for the first ten riders home in every race. Having said that, 10th place won you a paltry one pound. As in Coupe Kawasaki, there was a push-start, just to make life interesting.

A maximum of only 25 riders competed,

147

THE KAWASAKI TRIPLES BIBLE

Kawasaki dealership Bol d'Or-sponsored rider Neil Storey, who made a big impression in the '79 season, picking up a win at Donington Park.

with less of a turnout at some meetings in the debut '78 season. On the upside, the KH400 Cup was supported by many dealer team entries, with Harvey Owen, Cradley, Daytona, Knott Mill in Manchester, and many others backing riders.

The winner that year was Kenny Pinks, who won the overall £400 top prize, plus a new Life helmet. Kenny went on to race a TZ350 at National level, but, tragically, was later killed in an accident at work. George Siergiejew was second, with Pirelli UK engineer Phil Hetherington in third.

Tweaking the formula

Of course, just as in Coupe Kawasaki France, the UK series saw rules being bent, as ex-Kawasaki 400 racer Dave Matthews recalled. "I first competed in some of the rounds during the '78 season," said Dave, "and after hacking up, then welding

The UK KH400 Race Series

my exhausts, fitting rear sets and lower handlebars, I raced at Wellsbourne in the Midlands, Cadwell and Mallory. But it was obvious that some of the bikes were running tuned engines, with the heads skimmed and ports opened up. You couldn't get near them on the straights. Brian Flak, who ran a Kawasaki dealership in Kent back then, was tipped as the best man for that job so I had him tune my engine to make it competitive. It worked, the bike went much faster."

Apart from the number of rounds and geographical spread, one of the factors which held back the series was the choice of circuits. Wellsbourne near Stratford-on-Avon was a typical ex-WWII aerodrome, featuring a dubious track surface. "I recall following Phil Hetherington, who was one of the front runners in the KH400 series," said Dave Matthews, "and he actually crashed in front of me along the main straight! The bumps were so bad

An image from a UK market brochure for the B4 model.

Action from Lydden, one of the smaller circuits on the KH400 calendar.

you were bounced out of the saddle, it was horrendous."

During the '78 season, Kawasaki UK had made a race-kitted KH400 available to journalists who wanted to have a go for feature purposes, and Bob Goddard from *New Motorcycling Monthly* (*NMM*) was one. The publication was owned by IPC, a large, London-based publisher which also produced *Motor Cycle Weekly*, a rival to *MCN* at the time.

Building on this media connection, Kawasaki UK managed to expand the KH400 Cup to 19 rounds for 1979, bringing in *NMM* as title sponsor and getting a little contingency money from Shell, Speedman Leathers, Champion sparkplugs, Brands Hatch Race School, and Dunlop.

It was a smart move, as rival publisher EMAP had backed the Avon Roadrunner series in the mid '70s, which was overshadowing other production road racing series by some margin. KH400 Cup race winners in '79 could expect to net £12 for 1st place, plus £3 from any sponsor who had a sticker on their bike, or products used on the bike. But even if a rider won £24 on the day, this would barely cover travel expenses.

The UK KH400 Race Series

Waiting in the pit lane at Brands Hatch for what looks like a cold race, judging by the heavy coats worn by spectators.

It wasn't the ticket to the big time that the Coupe Kawasaki series was in France.

The '79 season got under way and Hetherington emerged as an early leader of the series, closely chased by Andy Pilgrim, who was also campaigning an RD400 in the Avon series. *Motor Cycle Weekly* sent Graham Sanderson along to Cadwell Park, who crashed his bike in practice and finished 20th. Sanderson described the KH400 series as making the then blockbuster Hollywood movie *Rollerball* "look like a vicarage tea party." His report was enlivened by a photo showing a multi-bike crash at the tricky Gooseneck corner on the circuit.

Phil Hetherington went on to win the '79 title, with Pilgrim second and Lincolnshire's Neil Storey making an impressive race debut in third.

For 1980, Kawasaki UK decided to have two classes: Class B for KH400s, and an Class A for the new Z500 four-strokes – with more prize money on offer for the 500 riders. For many, this was the beginning of the end, and left a sour taste for riders who had forked out quite a bit of money on their road/race KH400.

"I'd got into the Kawasaki race series by just buying a KH400 from a dealer and thinking 'Yeah, I'll have a go'" comments Dave Matthews, "I remember the weekend I bought the KH400, it was the same weekend that the new Z1R was launched, in March '78. My bike was maroon with red and orange stripes. The KH400 was taxed and road legal, so I did some running-in then paid eight quid to try open practice at Mallory. Somehow I managed to highside the bike – incredible on such a low-powered machine."

Things didn't go any better for Dave in the first race. "I went to Wellesbourne and got T-boned by a guy on a 250 Ducati. On another attempt I followed Kenny Pinks into a field as he out-braked himself. My results

151

The Kawasaki Triples Bible

Those who ran their KH400s in open class production races soon found that Yamaha's RD400 was faster and more nimble.

weren't great. When Kawasaki announced in '79 that the Z500 would be taking over as the main bike in the series, I realised I had a heavily modified road bike, which was pretty worthless in terms of re-sale value."

The main problem with the series was that it started too late. After '76, when the RD400 came out, the KH400 simply wasn't competitive. By '79 when machines like Suzuki's X7 250 could hit over 100mph with some porting work, the game was effectively up for the outdated triple.

"Nobody in the paddock wanted an uncompetitive 400 for club racing," comments Dave Matthews, "and no road rider wanted something with welded-on rear sets, a hacked-up set of exhausts, and a cut-down saddle. I got so disillusioned with racing that I went despatch riding in London instead."

During the 1980 season there were fewer riders on the KH400, and in '81 the series was entirely for Z500s as the KH400 had been officially dropped from the Kawasaki UK line-up back in '79, so Kawasaki UK wasn't interested in promoting the bikes any longer.

The series did spark an interest in one-make road racing in the UK, however, and the RD350LC Pro-Am Cup, which was televised in ITV's *World of Sport* in the early '80s demonstrated that the idea was simple. It provided brilliant, on-track entertainment when complete amateurs were pitted against up-and-coming professional racers, all on more or less equal machinery.

KH400 series collector's notes
Very few KH400s survived the series, and the sudden drop in values affected the race machines badly once it finished. Many bikes were worth less than £200, and simply broken up for spares.
Leading dealers who entered teams included Daytona of Ruislip, Bol d'Or of

These two bikes demonstrate typical modifications for racing. Standard exhausts have been bent inward, flat 'bars fitted, and a huge plate mounts the rear sets.

The late Kenny Pinks receives the champion's trophy for the '78 season title, with Phil Hetherington on the left and George Siergiejew on the right.

Lincoln, Harvey Owen, Boyer Racing, Cradley Heath Kawasaki in the West Midlands, and Kawasaki Carlisle. Some dealers ran two bikes in the series and had them painted in team colours, with Cradley Heath, Harvey Owen and Daytona amongst the most distinctive.

Green or green and white were popular colour choices for those who re-sprayed their bikes, but many riders, like frontrunner Phil Hetherington simply applied a few tickers to a stock Candy Royal Purple '78 KH400.

General modifications from standard on a KH400 Series race machine would include 'Ace' 'bars or clip-ons, sections of exhausts replaced with matt black pipework tucked in close to the engine, and race number boards at the front and on the sides. You were allowed to cut down the stock seat's interior padding, but not replace it. The grab rail was supposed to be removed, along with the indicators and stands. Some riders left the rails on, however; often, they rode home after the race! Lights had to be retained, but the brake light disconnected and lenses taped up in case of a crash.

Most KH400 racers had home-brewed rear sets and an elongated shift linkage fitted by the riders or dealerships. Most riders ran with Girling shocks rather than stock items, as replacement was allowed under the regulations. You could also change the front fork internals and run with a different set of sprockets.

One re-bore was allowed on the engine barrels, but no tuning. Most bikes had port work done, and squish bands altered on the cylinder heads to try and squeeze more power from the 400cc motor. Jets were obviously changed, too.

KH400 series 1978 results

Position	Rider	Points
1st	Kenny Pinks	206
2nd	George Siergiejew	192
3rd	Phil Hetherington	129
4th	Dave Parratt	90
5th	Jim Davidson	83
6th	Keith Ferrell	82
7th	Martin Howard-Hildige	49
8th=	Paul Berresford	40
8th=	Mike Woodward	40
10th=	Paul Busby	37
10th=	Ian Skinner	37

Motor Cycling KH400 series 1979 results

Position	Rider	Points
1st	Phil Hetherington	237
2nd	Andy Pilgrim	190
3rd	Neil Storey	147
4th	Dave Parratt	133
5th	Andrew Blackshaw	71
6th	Trevor Gordon	61
7th	Joe Maxwell	50
8th	Neil Williams	37
9th	Nicol Robb	36
10th	Clifton Tabiner	31

Visit Veloce on the web – www.veloce.co.uk / www.velocebooks.com
Details of all books in print • Special offers • New book news • Gift vouchers • Forum

ALSO FROM VELOCE PUBLISHING

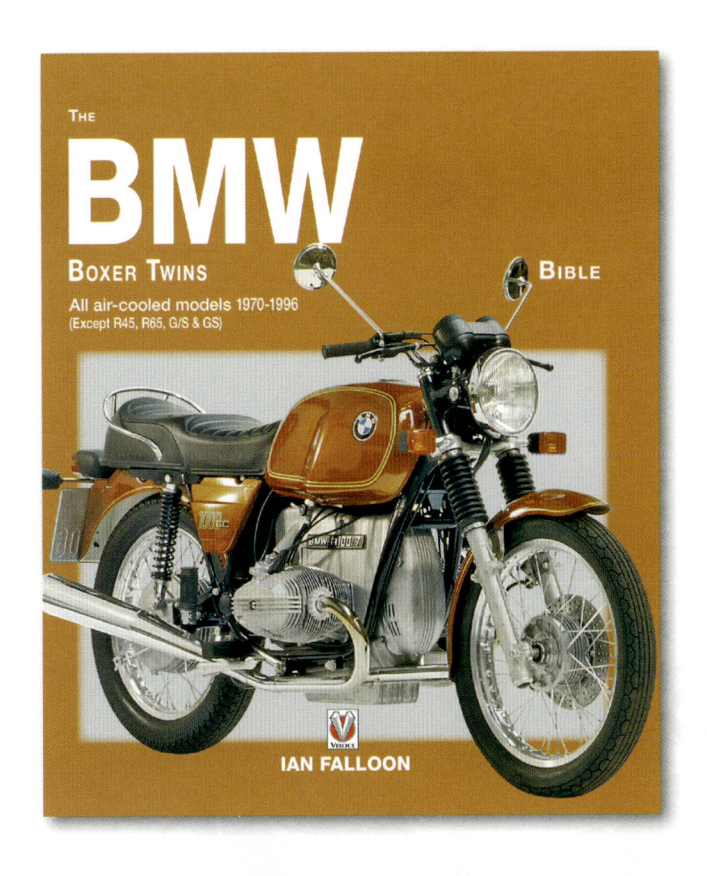

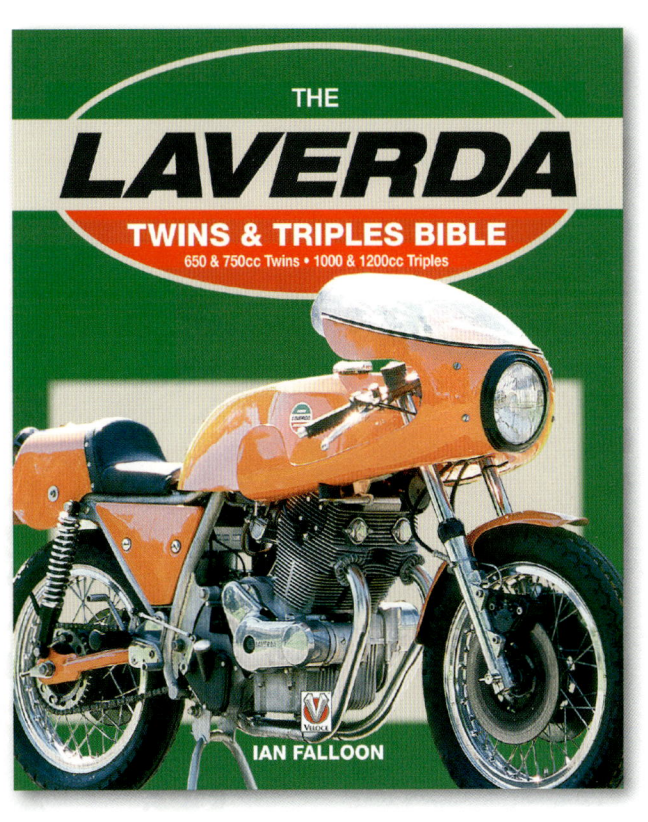

The BMW Boxer Twins Bible

- *Hardback*
- *25x20.7cm*
- *£29.99 / $59.95*
- *160 pages*
- *192 colour and b&w pictures*
- *ISBN: 978-1-84584-168-3*

The air-cooled boxer BMW twins were among the most significant motorcycles of the late 1970s and 1980s, providing an unparalleled combination of comfort, reliability, and performance. Written by a world-renowned motorcycle journalist and featuring 190 colour photographs, here is the authoritative work on these machines.

Laverda Twins & Triples Bible

- *Hardback*
- *25x20.7cm*
- *£29.99 / $59.95*
- *160 pages*
- *222 mainly colour photos*
- *ISBN: 978-1-845840-58-7*

The large capacity Laverda twins and triples were some of the most charismatic and exciting motorcycles produced in a golden era. With a successful endurance racing programme publicising them, Laverda's twins soon earned a reputation for durability. Here is the year-by-year, model-by-model, change-by-change record.

For more info on Veloce titles, visit our website at www.veloce.co.uk
email info@veloce.co.uk • Tel: +44 (0)1305 260068 • prices subject to change • p+p extra

ALSO FROM VELOCE PUBLISHING

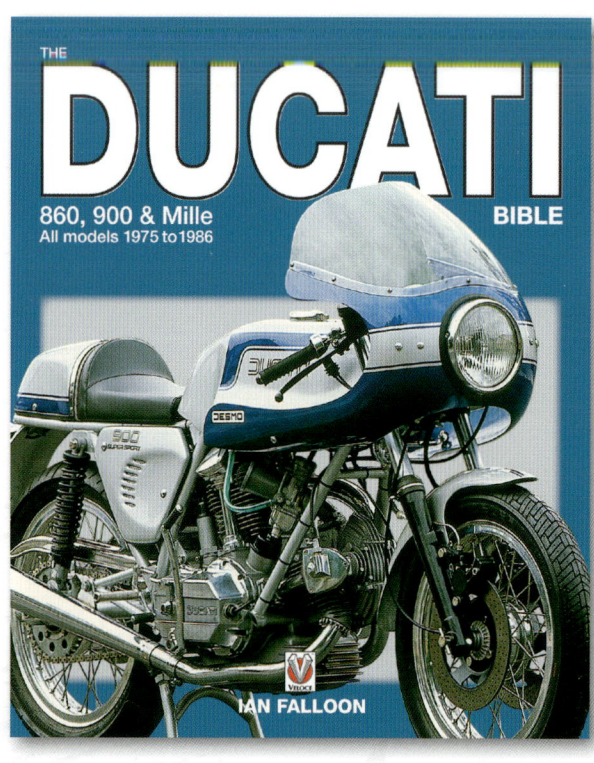

The Ducati 860, 900 & Mille Bible

- *Hardback*
- *25x20.7cm*
- *£29.99 / $59.95*
- *160 pages*
- *178 colour & b&w photos*
- *ISBN: 978-1-845841-21-8*

Covers all of the landmark Ducatis of the late 1970s to early 1980s, including the 900 Super Sport and Mike Hailwood replica. Highly illustrated and with complete appendices of technical specifications, this is a year-by-year, change-by-change guide. An absolute must-have for any Ducati aficionado.

The book of the Ducati 750 SS 'Round-case' 1974

- *Hardback*
- *25x25cm*
- *£40.00 / $79.95*
- *176 pages*
- *259 colour and b&w pictures*
- *ISBN: 978-1-84584-202-4*

Although manufactured for only one year, 1974, the Ducati 750 Super Sport was immediately touted as a future classic. It was a pioneer motorcycle – expensive and rare, and produced by Ducati's race department to celebrate victory in the 1972 Imola 200 Formula 750 race; for Ducatisti, it is the Holy Grail.

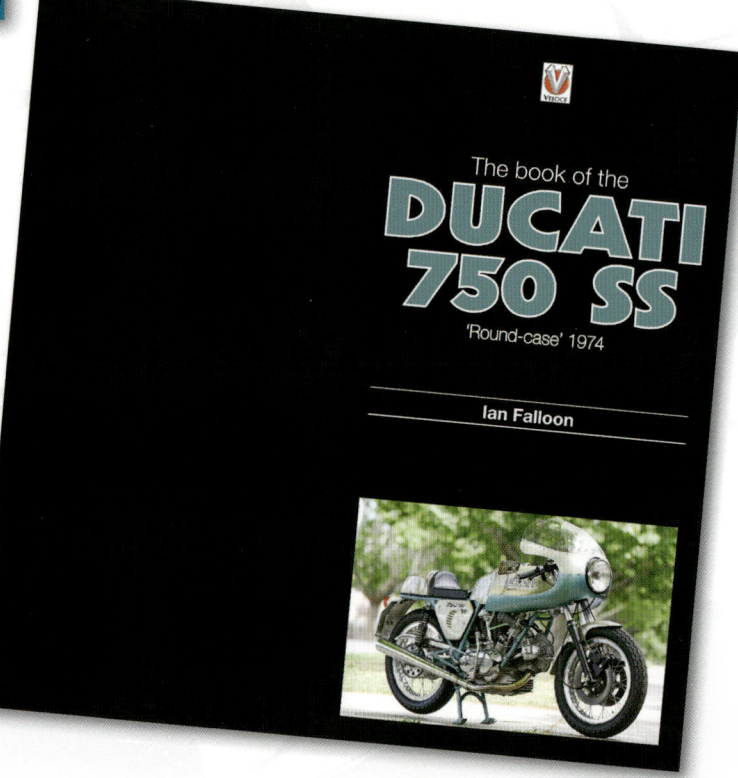

For more info on Veloce titles, visit our website at www.veloce.co.uk
email info@veloce.co.uk • Tel: +44 (0)1305 260068 • prices subject to change • p+p extra

ALSO FROM VELOCE PUBLISHING

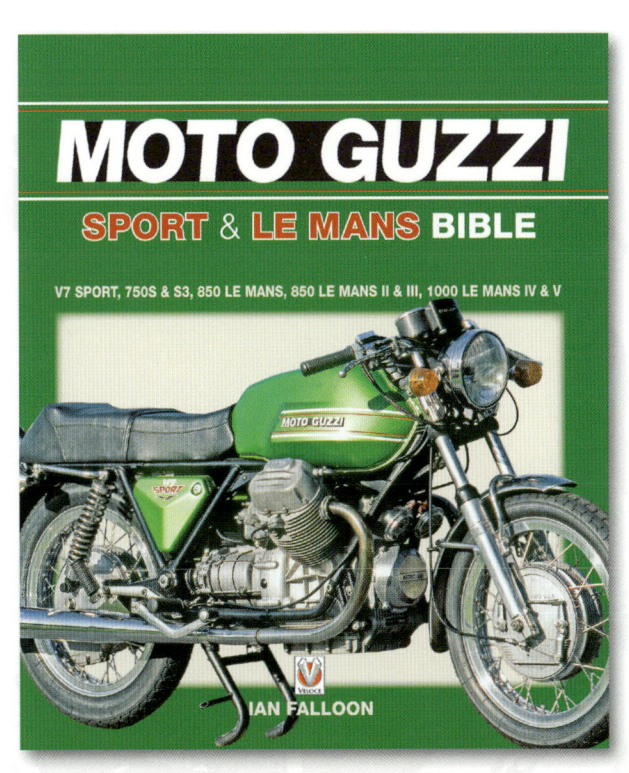

The Moto Guzzi Sport & Le Mans Bible

- *Hardback*
- *25x20.7cm*
- *£29.99 / $59.95*
- *160 pages*
- *160 colour and b&w pictures*
- *ISBN: 978-1-845840-64-8*

The Moto Guzzi V7 Sport and Le Mans are iconic sporting motorcycles of the 1970s and 1980s. Covering the period 1971-1993, and all models with a description of model development year-by-year, full production data and 160 photos, this is a highly informative book and an essential Bible for enthusiasts.

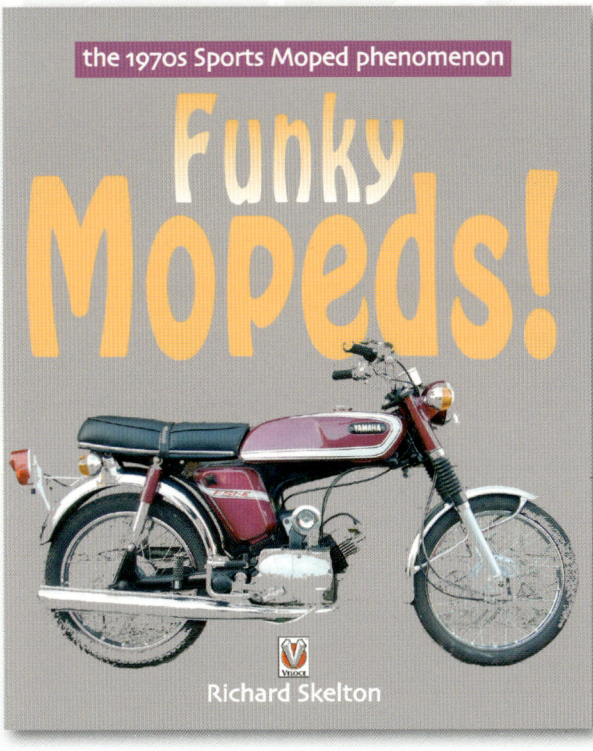

Funky mopeds

- *Paperback*
- *25x20.7cm*
- *£14.99 / $29.95*
- *144 pages*
- *ISBN: 978-1-845840-78-5*

A change in the British legal definition of a 'Moped' (motorcycle with pedals) led to an explosion of high-performance 50cc machines which were every teenager's dream during the 1970s. Here's a colourful celebration of those fantastic machines and the culture of the 1970s.

For more info on Veloce titles, visit our website at www.veloce.co.uk
email info@veloce.co.uk • Tel: +44 (0)1305 260068 • prices subject to change • p+p extra

Also from Veloce Publishing

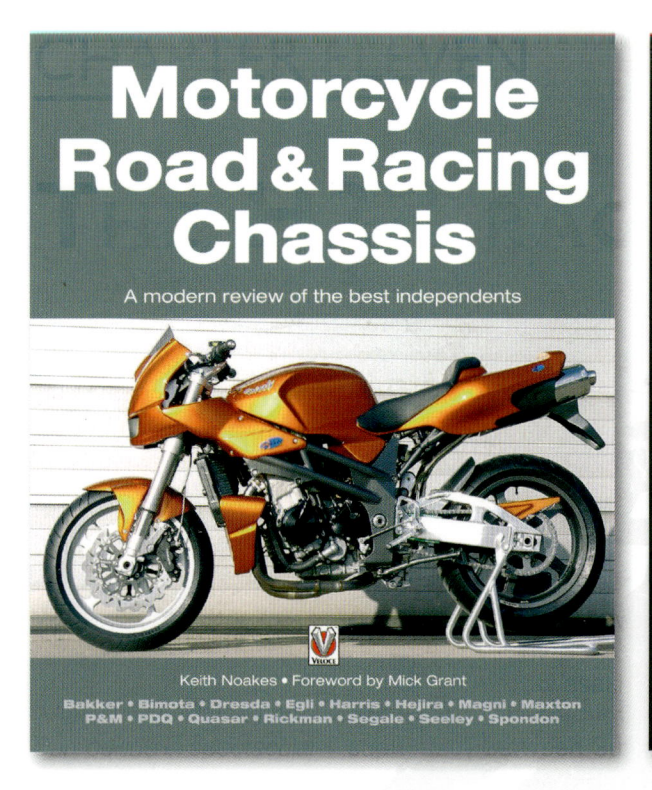

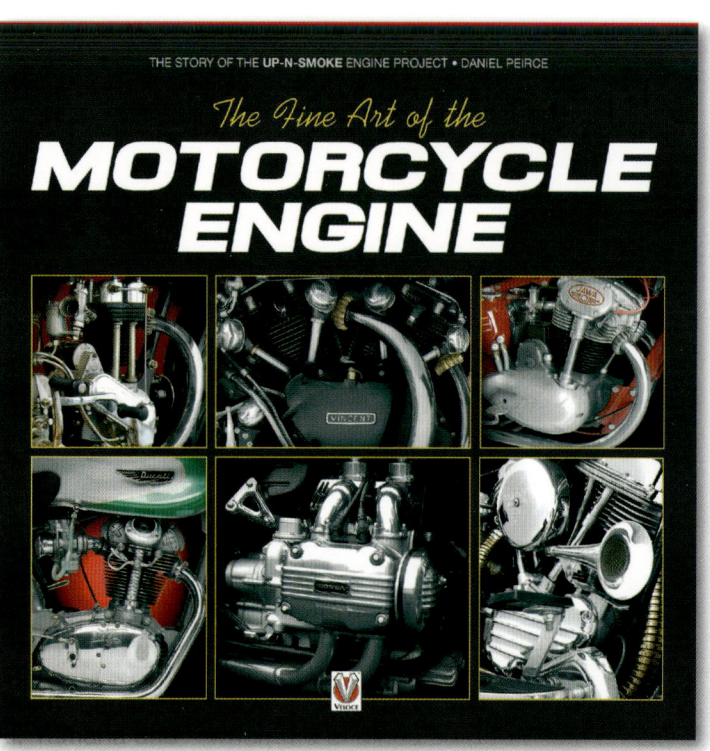

Motorcycle road & racing chassis

- *Paperback*
- *25x20.7cm*
- *£19.99 / £39.95*
- *176 pages*
- *246 colour and b&w pictures*
- *ISBN: 978-1-845841-30-0*

An account of the independent companies and individuals who have played a major part in the design and advancement of motorcycle frame (chassis) performance. With full specifications for many chassis and extensively illustrated throughout, this book is a must for any motorcycle enthusiast, and a valuable reference for the trade.

The fine art of the motorcycle engine

- *Hardback*
- *25x25cm*
- *£19.99 / £39.95*
- *144 pages*
- *90 colour pictures*
- *ISBN: 978-1-845841-74-4*

Professional photographer Dan Peirce presents 64 stunning pictures from his popular 'Up-n-Smoke' engine project. The book also tells the story behind the project and how it took years to bring it from an inspired idea to a tangible reality. "Pornography for Gearheads" – Cycle World magazine.

For more info on Veloce titles, visit our website at www.veloce.co.uk
email info@veloce.co.uk • Tel: +44 (0)1305 260068 • prices subject to change • p+p extra

INDEX

Agrati Sales 32, 93, 96
American Eagle 350 19
Avenger 350 12-14, 17, 139, 140

Ballington, Kork 87, 107
Baranne, Daniel 23
Baumann, Art 131-133
Boddice, Mick 115, 116
Bradley, Rusty 119, 125, 126
Brett, Rick 35, 50, 66

Cameron, Kevin 68, 125, 126, 132, 138
Chapman, Colin 118
Croxford, Dave 118
Crussell, Dave 129

Davick Motique 78, 90, 102
DKW 9, 16
Du Hamel, Yvon 121, 131, 135, 138
Dunnell, Tony 112, 113
Dyson, Ian 109, 110

Flak, Brian 34, 149

Hacking, Doug 77, 107
Hall, Randy 130, 135
Hansen, Bob/Team 114, 121, 129, 130, 135
Hansford, Gregg 117
Hetherington, Phil 148, 149, 151, 153
Honda, Soichiro 8, 9, 16

Jakeman, Tony 86, 144, 145

Kawasaki Aircraft 8
Koup, Larry 123, 124

Lister, Simon 79
Louis, Detlev 32, 80, 102

Meguro 10
Meihatsu 8, 9
Maugendre, Xavier 22, 23, 32, 71, 139, 142
Mitsubishi 26-28
Molloy, Ginger 117
Moran, Ed 25, 29, 122

Nicosia, Tony 25
Nixon, Gary 126, 131, 133, 136
Norman, John 95, 96
Norwich Union 85

Offenstadt, Eric 117, 118, 128, 133

Penney, Bill 112
Pilgrim, Andy 151
Pinks, Kenny 148, 151, 153
Pons, Patrick 141, 142
Pridmore, Reg 113
Pro-Am Cup 152

Ravel, Christian 118
Renolds chain 114

Index

Rikuo 10

Samurai 250 12-15, 139
Sanderson, Graham 151
Sarron, Christian 139, 141
Saul, Eric 139, 141
Sayle, Murray 136
Seeley, Colin 130, 131
Sheene, Barry 103
Shenton, Stan 95, 128
Siergiejew, George 148, 153
Simmonds, Dave 13, 14, 115, 116

Smart, Paul 129-131
Smith, Bill 21, 96, 112, 114
Sprayson, Ken 115
Steele, Phil 33, 34
Storey, Neil 148
Suzuki X7 104, 152

Tait, Percy 112

Uphill, Malcolm 112

Vink, Henk 24, 25